Bryan Lask, LRCP, MRCS, MB, BS, M.Phil, MRC Psych is Consultant Psychiatrist at the world-famous Hospital for Sick Children, Great Ormond Street in London, and Honorary Lecturer at London University's Institute of Child Health. He is a Member of the Royal Society of Medicine and the British Paediatric Association, as well as being Council Member of the Association for Family Therapy and the Association for Child Psychology and Psychiatry.

Dr Lask is well-known around the world for his clinical and research work into childhood behavioural problems. He has addressed international meetings in the United States and several European countries; was Visiting Professor to the University of British Columbia in Canada; and has spent time as Visiting Professor at the Universities of North Carolina and Kentucky in the United States.

In addition, Dr Lask is Editor of the *Journal of Family Therapy*, Assessor for the *British Medical Journal*, and has published numerous specialist medical papers and articles.

Dr Lask is married and has two children.

 POSITIVE HEALTH GUIDE

OVERCOMING BEHAVIOR PROBLEMS IN CHILDREN
A practical guide

Bryan Lask, MD

Foreword by
Professor Al Solnit,
Professor of Child Psychiatry,
Yale Child Studies Center, New Haven

Arco Publishing, Inc.
New York

Dedicated to Judith
with love and gratitude

Published in 1985 by Arco Publishing, Inc
215 Park Avenue South, New York, NY 10003

First published in the United Kingdom in 1985
by Martin Dunitz Ltd, London.

Library of Congress Cataloging in Publication Data
Lask, Bryan.
   Overcoming behavior problems in children.
   (Positive health guide)
   Includes index.
   1. Child rearing.   2. Child psychology.
3. Adolescent psychology.   4. Problem children.
I. Title.   II. Series.
HQ769.L313 1985   649'.153   84-24552
ISBN 0-668-06378-5

Phototypeset in Garamond by Book Ens, Saffron Walden, Essex
Printed by Toppan Printing Company (S) Pte Ltd, Singapore

CONTENTS

£6.95

FOREWORD

Albert J. Solnit, M.D.
Sterling Professor of Pediatrics and Psychiatry
Yale University, New Haven, Connecticut.

Overcoming Behavior Problems in Children gives the reader a balanced perspective on child life and development. Dr Lask explains the ways in which early life reflects a child's endowment and experience. He calls the reader's attention to sizing up children's strengths and weaknesses at various stages in their development in the context of the family, the community and the child's culture.

With a sensitive, realistic edge towards optimistic expectations, Dr Lask uses his knowledge to enhance and strengthen parents' capacity to understand and act for their children. In language and concept, the author has written effectively for English-reading parents and their supporters the world over. He has that rare talent of both knowing and conveying how the child views his plight; and how his parents feel about the commonest difficulties experienced by their children at the best and worst of times. Writing lucidly about the complexity of healthy development, its detours and its obstacles, Dr Lask brings the whole child into the picture so parents as well as teachers, nurses, family physicians, psychologists, social and child care workers can tune into the 'difficult' child with compassionate understand-

ing. This book guides these adults in applying an appropriately active role to help the child cope with his symptomatic emotional and behavioral problems and to resume progressive, healthy functioning and development.

Though the author has enabled the reader to know the incidence and range of childhood mental and emotional difficulties, he reflects on these figures in a painless and illuminating way, never confusing statistics with the uniqueness of each child and his particular problems. Dr Lask uses common sense to relate the wisdom of ordinary devoted parents to our best knowledge about children in the 1980s. Thus, this book has a future because the author has provided a text about children that is clear, interesting and at a level of explanation that avoids dogma while remaining open to the continuing process of revision and expansion to our existing knowledge.

Throughout the book, Dr Lask recognizes that parents are the ultimate experts in the care of their children and he has provided parents, and all who wish to add a balanced understanding to their relationships with children, with a sensible child-health guidebook.

INTRODUCTION

As a parent there are many occasions over the years when you may worry about your children. Sometimes the worry is small and disappears of its own accord; at other times you may be more seriously concerned. Indeed, it would be very unusual if you never worried about your children. It may be reassuring to know that other children have the same problems as your own, and that other parents have shared the same worries.

It is often said that bringing up children is the most difficult job in the world, and it is important to remember that it is impossible to do it perfectly. Children need to experience their parents being less than perfect so that they themselves can cope with frustration, unhappiness, worries or arguments. Parents often make mistakes, get fed up, feel overwhelmed, lose their temper, or want to be left alone. There is no need to feel badly if you are not always calm, attentive and loving. No-one can be that way all the time.

In this book I describe the main behavioural, emotional and developmental problems that children experience, and try to guide the reader through them, hopefully, to a successful outcome. I explain what kind of problems should be serious causes for concern and compare these with normal, transient difficulties. I discuss what you can do to help your child, emphasizing the importance of trying to understand him and seeing things from his point of view, but never forgetting that parents cannot devote all their time and energy to their children.

I have used many examples of real problems faced by families, but although the main content of the examples is true, I have changed the names and some details so that no-one can be recognized. The examples serve to put childhood problems into perspective, for although they are dealt with individually in the book, your child may well be experiencing more than one problem at the same time.

I have used the pronoun 'he' all the way through (except when 'she' is appropriate) for ease of reading, but of course girls have problems too, and it, in no way, reflects a higher regard for one sex than the other. The few drugs mentioned in the text are referred to by their generic (pharmaceutical) names only. A table of British, American, Canadian and Australian tradenames has been included at the end of the book.

You can read this book straight through, dip in to it, or look up a specific problem you are experiencing at the time. This book is designed so that you can do any of these with relative ease. Although no-one is a perfect parent, you are obviously a caring and concerned one, and I hope you find the book a useful aid to doing a very important, though sometimes difficult, exhausting and over-whelming job.

In the first half of the book I talk about the common problems affecting children from the first day of life, through school and into early adolescence, whether they are difficulties with feeding, sleeping, toilet-training and bad behaviour, or hyperactivity, clumsiness and psychosomatic problems– to name but a few examples. Later I introduce the concept of good-enough parenting – the ability of both parents to recognize and respond to the child's needs, and discuss where to seek help for a particular problem, and what to expect the various professions to say and do. But first, of course, we need to know how to recognize a problem, to understand how it arose in the first place and how to start tackling it.

1. DOES YOUR CHILD HAVE PROBLEMS?

Bringing up children is a complicated and tiring experience, but it can also be great fun and very rewarding. It is ironic that despite the fact that it is one of the most important jobs anyone ever does, it does not receive that recognition, and there is virtually no training available!

Children can be loveable one moment, and thoroughly disagreeable the next; they can be the source of immense joy but the cause of much frustration and irritation; they can make enormous demands on their parents but equally they can give you unconditional love and an immeasureable sense of importance.

It is inevitable that as parents you will worry from time to time when you suspect that your child may have serious problems. But all children occasionally have difficulties; most are fortunately mild and short-lived. Some, however, are more serious or long-lasting. In this chapter I want to discuss how to tell whether your child's behaviour is anything to worry about, look at how often and why problem behaviour arises. In later chapters I shall discuss in more detail many of the particular problems of childhood and how you can help your child overcome them.

How do you know whether your child has problems?

Because so much childhood behaviour can be worrying, you will need to be able to tell the difference between what is a temporary bit of odd behaviour, an ordinary difficulty, and what is a real problem. To illustrate how you can do this, consider the behaviour of these two young boys.

Neil, aged seven, had never really been a problem, according to his parents. He had plenty of friends, was getting on well at school, and seemed happy at home. Occasionally he wet his bed, and sometimes would lose his temper and rush out of the room, or go into a sulk for an hour or two. Every so often he would pick a fight with his younger brother, refuse to do as he was told, or tell lies. Most days he had a good appetite and most nights he slept well, but occasionally he would go off his food, or sleep badly.

Neil was in no way a disturbed or problem child. He simply showed the variations in behaviour that are part of normal, healthy development. These are ordinary difficulties, not real problems. His parents recognized this and made no effort to change him. If they had, they might have made a problem out of nothing (see Chapter nine, on the ins and outs of parenting).

Roy was also seven. He, too, had plenty of friends, and did well with his school work, although he was often in trouble with his teacher for being naughty He could be quite naughty at home, too, and his parents would have to tell him many times to stop doing something before he would take any notice. Most nights he refused to go to bed, and if taken to his room would run out as soon as he was left. On a number of occasions he had walked out of the house, and was some way from home before his anxious mother found him. He often teased the cat and once his mother caught him putting the cat in the washing-machine.

In contrast to Neil, Roy's behaviour did give cause for concern. He was continually doing many things that were defiant, and some that were destructive. Roy's parents were right to bring him along so that we could sort out what was behind the bad behaviour.

In trying to work out whether your child does have real problems, you need to ask a number of questions:

1. How many different things is he doing that worry you?
2. How frequently does he do things that worry you?
3. Is his behaviour dangerous, destructive or aggressive, either to himself or others?
4. Is he in obvious distress?

The more things he does that worry you, the more likely it is that he has real problems. If his behaviour is dangerous, destructive or aggressive, you really should be concerned, and the same applies if you can see that something is obviously worrying or upsetting him.

What is normal at one age can be a problem at another

An important point to remember is that you should expect different behaviour at different ages. A particular type of behaviour, however tiresome, may be quite normal at one age, and yet could be the sign of a problem at another.

For example, a two-year-old child is behaving normally when he becomes upset if his mother leaves him with a stranger. A five-year-old generally copes with being at school, away from his mother, for at least half of each day. Not that there is anything unusual, nor is it a sign of disturbance, if there are occasional tears or clinging. However, by the age of eight, such behaviour would be distinctly unusual and certainly a cause for concern.

Another example is that of naughtiness or mischievousness. Two-year-olds quite naturally and healthily test the limits of their parents' endurance. They have to learn what is permissable and what is not. School-age children are also likely to be mischievous. There is nothing unhealthy about this, but you would expect your school-age child to know the difference between right and wrong. He may quite naturally test the limits but not as frequently as a toddler, and most of the time he should be able to set certain limits on his naughtiness himself. Adolescence is a time when there is rebellion against parental values and attitudes. Teenagers do more than test the limits, they break them! This can be upsetting, worrying or infuriating to us as parents. The only consolation is that nearly all adolescents do so.

How common are the problems of childhood?

There is no simple answer to this question. As I stated earlier, virtually all children have problems from time to time. Serious problems, which require some form of outside advice or treatment, affect around 10 to 20 per cent of children in such countries as Britain, North America, Australia and New Zealand. In the following chapters I will give some indication of how often particular problems such as bed-wetting, phobias or refusal to go to school occur.

How do problems arise?

There are many things in your child's life that can influence his chances of developing a problem. Often a problem can be produced by a combination of factors. These include:

- Temperament
- The inherited tendency to experience particular problems
- Parental handling
- Family difficulties
- Life's stresses
- Illness
- Handicap.

Let us see how each of these can contribute:

Temperament

Every child is born with his or her own temperament, that is certain characteristics such as calmness or excitability; adaptability (how readily he can adapt to change or stress); a tendency to worry or remain calm; a particular level of activity; and so on. These characteristics are more or less laid down for your child while he is still in the womb and do not change much. A child who tends to be excitable, irritable and anxious will obviously experience life differently from a child who is calm and placid. It is for this reason that two children from the same family with similar life experiences (even identical experiences, for that matter), can turn out so differently. Parents often say to me something like, 'But I handle him exactly the same as the others, so

why is he so difficult when the others aren't?'. Differences in temperament go a long way to explaining this.

Inherited problems

As well as inheriting temperament, children can also inherit a tendency to develop certain problems, such as bed-wetting, reading difficulties (dyslexia) and anxiety. Children who have any of these or other problems often have parents or brothers and sisters who have had similar difficulties. This is because these problems are inherited in the same way as such things as blue eyes, being very tall, or being good at music are also inherited.

Parental handling

Fortunately, despite a lack of training or experience, most parents seem to get it right most of the time. Mistakes are made, but children are generally remarkably resilient. So long as we, as parents, are able to learn from our mistakes, no great damage is done.

Occasionally, however, some parents do continually or too often get it wrong. When this happens, problems are likely to arise. What type of problem arises and how serious it can become depends on a number of factors, such as family difficulties, all kinds of stress and illness and handicaps. I shall mention them here briefly and deal with them in more detail in later chapters.

In Chapter nine, for instance, I shall discuss in detail the ins and outs of parenting and you should refer to that chapter if you want to check on what to do in various situations.

Family difficulties

The family is the single most important part of a child's life. A good family life is beyond value. Sadly, when things go wrong in families this can have a bad effect on the child. Some obvious examples are when parents are having problems with their marriage, money worries or other stresses such as poor housing, illness or death in the family, and so on.

Incidentally, it's worth noting that a good family life has far more to it than simply providing plenty of love and attention. Children need to learn how to cope with discipline, disappointment, separation, and arguments. You must provide your child with the opportunity to learn how to handle such situations or he will be ill-equipped to cope with life.

Often parents say to me 'We're a very close family', or 'We never have a cross word', or 'We always avoid disappointments'. Well-intentioned though such ideas are, they will not help your child to cope when the time comes for him to be away from his family, or when an argument does arise, or he has to be disciplined, or disappointment can't be avoided. The answer lies in providing a healthy balance – moderation in all things!

All these points are discussed in more detail in Chapters eight and nine.

Life's stresses

Life is full of stresses. From a very early age, children are exposed to unavoidable stresses. Early examples could be the birth of a brother or sister, or ill health. Then comes starting school, the breaking-up of friendships and later leaving home, finding a job, and so on. These cannot be avoided, nor should they be. Whether they create problems for your child will depend on how he is able to cope with them, upon you being able to

The family is the single most important part of a child's life.

help, or even calling in specialized help (see Chapter ten).

Incidentally, there is a myth that to be the middle child is more stressful than the eldest or youngest (sometimes called 'pig-in-the-middle'). This is not so – there is no such thing as a middle-child syndrome. It is no more or less stressful being the eldest, middle or youngest. It is possible, however, that *only* children are more vulnerable, as they partially miss out on the opportunity to learn about close relationships, sharing, quarrelling and so on.

Illness and handicap

If you have a child with a recurring or long-lasting illness, such as asthma, or diabetes, then he is about twice as likely as a healthy child to develop problems. Children who have an illness such as epilepsy, or who are mentally or physically handicapped, are even more likely to develop problems. This is hardly surprising as life is bound to be more difficult for them and for their parents. The problems connected with such disabilities are dealt with in Chapters six and seven.

How different factors can combine

We have looked at a number of factors that can lead to problems developing in your child. The chances are, though, that problems are more likely to be caused by a combination of factors. I remember this case of a five-year-old boy:

Edward started wetting his bed after having been dry at night since the age of two and a half.

When I talked to his parents they gave me some interesting information: his father and two uncles had all been bed-wetters. Also, Edward had always been a worrier and found separation from his mother difficult. Because of this she had tended to avoid situations where he had to be apart from her. His parents also told me that they were under a lot of tension because of the possibility of Edward's father becoming unemployed. Finally, Edward was about to start school.

In Edward's case you can see how temperament (tendency to worry), inheritance (three people in the family had been bed-wetters), parental handling (mother's overprotectiveness), family difficulties (tensions around unemployment) and life stresses (starting school) have all combined. The outcome is that Edward started wetting his bed.

Often, it is only necessary for a couple of these factors to combine to produce a problem. What is most important is to recognize that when problems do arise, they usually have more than one cause.

What should you do if your child has a problem?

That is really what this book is about. Obviously, you want to sort it out as quickly and effectively as possible. In this chapter I have given you some idea of how a problem can arise. In later chapters I shall deal with particular problems and give hints about what you can do to overcome them. In my experience, many difficulties are overcome when parents change the way they handle their children (Chapter nine). If, after reading this book you are still worried about your child, yourself, or any other aspect of family life, including your marriage, you should not hesitate to seek the professional help I have discussed in Chapter ten.

2. PRE-SCHOOL PROBLEMS

In the early years of life there are many different emotional and behavioural problems that can occur. These can often be very upsetting both to the child and to the parents. Usually they are simply part of normal development and, handled appropriately, rapidly disappear. Sometimes, even if at first they are part of normal growing up, they can drag on. It may mean that your child is not coping with the problem and it is upsetting him.

In this chapter I look at problems that can occur in different areas of your child's life:

- Feeding problems
- Sleeping problems
- Toilet-training problems
- Habits
- Aggressive behaviour.

Although the problems listed here are more common in the pre-school years, they can also occur in later years as well. The way you go about tackling a problem tends to be the same whatever the age, though the older your child is, the more effort you should make to help him discuss his problem with you; then you can find the underlying causes and look for the possible solutions. If a problem should be tackled differently at a different age, I will specify the differences.

Feeding problems

Feeding your child is one of the closest and most important aspects of your relationship with him. Usually it is a rewarding and enjoyable experience. Unfortunately, difficulties sometimes arise. When they do, they can make parents very worried and anxious for reassurance. Problems that can occur in early life include:

- refusal to feed
- poor feeding
- restlessness during feeds
- crying during or between feeds
- vomiting
- diarrhoea
- failure to grow
- excess feeding
- obesity.

As your child gets older food fads may arise, and battles over food may become a major feature of your family life.

Feeding problems can be better tackled if we look firstly at what are considered normal feeding patterns and then at why problems may arise, how commonly they occur, when you should be concerned, and what you can do to overcome difficulties.

What is normal?
Babies are born with the ability to find, and suckle from their mother's nipple or a bottle nipple. Babies vary

15

Feeding, whether breast or bottle helps to establish a close and important bond between the mother and child.

enormously in how often they need feeding, how quickly they suckle, and how excited or calm they may be during feeding. You need not be surprised if your baby demands to be fed every two hours during the first two weeks, gulps it down at a dramatic speed, or appears easily distracted or fidgety during the feed. Equally, your child may quickly settle into a four-hourly routine, feed very slowly, or show little interest. Any combination of these features can occur and does not necessarily mean that there is a problem.

Finding the right routine for your baby
Most babies settle to a routine of four-hourly feeds a few weeks after birth, though again there is considerable variation. Some perfectly healthy babies seem to need feeding more frequently, others less frequently.

Breast-fed babies tend to need more frequent feeds than bottle-fed babies. This is not because their mothers are producing insufficient milk, but because breast-milk is less rich than artificial milk, therefore making more frequent feeds necessary. Nonetheless, research has made it clear that breast milk is generally better for a baby's physical health than artificial feeds. What is most important, however, is that you should feel comfortable with this method of feeding. If you prefer to bottle-feed this is perfectly all right, and you have no need to feel badly about it.

By the age of three to four months, most babies can swallow small amounts of solid food placed on the back of the tongue. Once again, babies are individuals like the rest of us, and some take longer before they are ready. As they grow, babies are able to cope with the wider range and larger quantity of food they need.

Why do feeding problems arise?

There are several possibilities why feeding problems arise. I shall group them under the following headings:

- temperamental variations
- problems during labour and shortly after birth
- emotional difficulties
- wrong quantity of food
- wrong type of food
- wrong feeding technique.

Temperamental variations Some babies are calm, placid and easy to care for; there is rarely a problem with feeding. Other babies are highly excitable, restless, easily distracted and find it hard to settle down to a feed. If your baby has that sort of temperament, then it is important to remain calm, tolerant and patient, or he may sense your anxiety or impatience and begin to associate feeding with an unpleasant sensation. You may then have a reluctant feeder on your hands.

Another group of babies just seem to be born reluctant feeders. From birth they appear to have poor appetites, and little interest in food. They tend to want minute amounts, and take a long time about it. If your baby fits into this category you will need saint-like patience to cope (see page 19).

Some babies seem to get into a sort of power struggle with their mothers. They want to feed in their own way and in their own time, whereas you want to fit his feeds into your own busy routine. This is a battle that you are likely to lose. I always advise parents to adapt to their baby – no harm is done and life becomes easier as a result!

Problems during labour and shortly after birth The kind of labour, delivery and early postnatal period you experience will affect feeding patterns. If the giving-birth period is lengthy and the medicines used are very powerful, then there is more likelihood of feeding difficulties. Premature babies, incidentally, make little demand for food and therefore need encouragement. Babies who are physically unwell have poorer appetites. In contrast, babies who are put to the breast immediately after delivery seem to take very well to breast-feeding.

Emotional difficulties For many different reasons, mothers can become depressed, anxious or in other ways upset. Babies can be very sensitive to the mood of their mothers. If, for example, you are feeling very tense while feeding this is somehow communicated to your baby and he may also become tense. He then unknowingly links feeding with the unpleasant sensation of tension and may become irritable during feeds and even lose interest. Not all babies react in this way. Many who seem to have bouncy, tough little personalities are quite oblivious to everything except the teat or nipple! As children get older, their own reactions to various upsets can affect their appetite. Some go off their food, while others react by over-eating.

The quantity of food may be wrong Inadequate amounts of food can leave your baby hungry and miserable. He may show this at the time by crying and restlessness. In the long run he may fail to grow adequately. Too much feed may lead to refusal to finish, vomiting and, in the end, obesity.

The type of food may be wrong The most likely problem here is the too-early introduction of solid feeds. If your baby is not yet able to digest them, he may cry or react against them with vomiting and diarrhoea. Some babies are sensitive or allergic to certain foods such as cow's milk, or eggs, but this problem is not as common as many people believe. If your baby does have a food allergy, then this may well cause vomiting and diarrhoea, pain and skin rashes. When the particular food that is causing the problem is left out of his diet all the symptoms will clear up. If you think your child may have an allergy, then do consult your doctor.

The way you feed your baby may be wrong A number of problems can be caused by the way you feed your baby. The breast may block your baby's nose, or he may not be held comfortably; the bottle may be held at the wrong angle, the hole in the teat may be too small or too large, or the milk may have been prepared incorrectly. Any of these can give rise to feeding difficulties.

How frequent are feeding difficulties?

Feeding problems occur most often in the first year of life. Indeed, most babies will from time to time go off their feeds, or occasionally vomit or have diarrhoea. These periods are usually very short-lived and need not be a cause for concern. It is not unusual for feeding difficulties to remain a common problem between the ages of one to five. Up to 50 per cent of children in this age range develop food fads or fussiness. Occasionally, school-age children may start eating too little or too much. This is discussed in later chapters.

When should you be concerned?

This depends partly on the age of your child. The younger the child, the more worrying it can be. Young babies who vomit or have diarrhoea for more than twelve hours should certainly be seen by a doctor because they cannot manage without the body fluids they are losing and may become dehydrated. On the other hand, a twenty-four hour episode in a much older child (two years and over) is unlikely to be so serious. The older child who is off his food may also be unwell, but unless there are other symptoms, he is unlikely to come to any harm.

Food fads are usually harmless. They are best ignored unless your child allows himself such a poor variety of foods that he is not growing. This is likely to be extremely rare. Even if it looks as though he's eating only fish fingers (sticks) or potato crisps (chips), the chances are that he is, unnoticed, eating other things too. Try, gently, to tempt him to eat other foods. Normally fads disappear within a few months. But, if you are in doubt, check with your doctor or a dietitian. Refusal to eat, or eating such small amounts that your child's growth is affected, is a serious matter, and a doctor's advice should be sought.

Excess eating to the point where your child is overweight or even obese can turn out to be harmful. This is because such eating patterns tend to last into adult life and, as we know from medical research, can cause physical ill-health, for example, heart disease. It is important to try and alter such habits as early as possible. Incidentally, overeating is never due to some form of illness or glandular disorder – it is simply a bad habit, that can become an addiction.

Regurgitation In the hospital where I work, we see between fifteen and twenty children a year who bring their food back into their mouths from their stomachs. Before a child regurgitates (sometimes called rumination) he often makes chewing motions, movements with his tongue or puts his fingers in his mouth and chews on them. It is as if the child can bring back his food at will. If this happens more than a few times you should take it seriously. It usually means something is wrong emotionally. If left untreated, it can lead to poor growth and eventually serious ill health.

What you can do to help

How you tackle feeding difficulties depends on the age of your child and the type of problem. Let us start with difficulties in the first year of life, and then deal with those in later years.

First year of life

Whatever the problem, remember that feeding takes time and patience. You and your baby need to feel relaxed and comfortable. Any attempt to rush is likely to create rather than overcome problems. If your baby is a very slow feeder, then these points become all the more important. If he frequently refuses feeds, or often seems reluctant, then you should check certain points:

The bottle feed – is it made correctly? Is it at the correct temperature? Is the bottle held at an angle that does not obstruct the nipple? Is the hole in the nipple the right size? (i.e. does it allow a drop of milk to come out each time the bottle is held upside-down and shaken).

Your baby – has he been burped satisfactorily? If he cries a lot during feeds then this is particularly important. If he cries after feeds, then you should also make sure that he is not suffering from gas.

How much feed – is it possible that he is not getting enough food? If such problems arise during breast-feeding, then again you should make sure that you are both comfortable, and that your breast is not blocking your baby's nose. He needs to be burped. Remember that with breast-feeding you will need to feed more frequently. If you have any doubts about the adequacy of the feeds, regular weighing will show whether or not your doubts are justified.

If problems still remain despite checking these points, then consult your health visitor (community nurse or public health nurse), nurse, or family doctor. They will be able to advise you on how to overcome the problem.

Some frequent worries

I am often asked which is better, breast- or bottle-feeding, demand- or schedule-feeding, and when should weaning start?

Breast or bottle? There is no doubt that breast-feeding is better than bottle-feeding. However, some mothers do not want to breast-feed, either for emotional or practical reasons. If you feel that way, then do not let anyone bully you into breast-feeding; you will feel resentful, you will not enjoy it, and anyhow it may not work. Incidentally, the most common cause for breast milk 'drying up' in the early weeks is the mother's anxiety or concern about breast-feeding. Family doctors can be very helpful in discussing these problems.

Demand or schedule? I am quite certain that demand-feeding is better, because it satisfies your baby's needs (an all-important consideration in early life). Most babies do develop a regular schedule after a few months. Schedule-feeding may be more convenient for the parents, but as I pointed out earlier, if you want an easy life with your baby it is better to organize yourself around him, rather than trying to get him to fit into your schedule. Some babies settle happily into the family timetable, but many do not!

A point of caution with regard to demand-feeding. Do make sure that it is a feed your baby needs, and not burping, or a diaper change, or simply a cuddle. If, each time your baby is upset or wanting attention or stimulation, he is fed, then very soon he will get into the habit of feeding to control distress. This is one sure way to overeating and eventual obesity.

When to wean? There is no need to wean before five months. You can introduce very small amounts of puréed foods before then, but it really isn't necessary and no advantage is gained by so doing.

How to handle feeding problems in toddlers and older children
Food fads are a part of normal development and should be ignored unless your child so restricts his diet that his health is threatened or his growth is delayed. If this is the case, you should discuss it with your family doctor. The same applies to rumination, food-refusal or extreme reluctance to feed. The more fuss you make, the more likely that the problem will remain.

Look for the source
Since the most common cause of feeding difficulties is some form of emotional upset, you should do your best to identify the source of this. Some children require far more attention and affection than others; if they don't get as much as they need they find other ways of satisfying themselves. Difficult feeding certainly involves the child getting additional attention – though not always the affection! Nevertheless, most children grow out of their feeding difficulties by the time they're six or seven.

A final point – don't class messy-eating as a problem. Most young children are messy eaters. They cannot help this, because eating does require skilled co-ordination, which is only achieved around the age of four or five years. You can help and encourage your child to guide most of his food into his mouth, but if you make a fuss about food going elsewhere, you are likely to create rather than solve problems. Children learn to eat tidily in time, and there is no point in expecting 'perfect' table manners before the age of seven at the earliest. If you suspect your child is being deliberately naughty with his food, set limits as to how far he can go with his mess, but don't show too much concern, or he may keep it up!

Sleeping problems

One of the most exhausting aspects of bringing up young children is that so often their, and consequently your, sleep is interrupted. Many children in the first four years of life develop sleep problems. Most babies wake frequently in the night during the first few months, and it is only as your child approaches his first birthday that you can expect more uninterrupted nights. The problem is so

It is normal for young children to make a mess when they eat.

common that we have even started a special sleep clinic in the hospital where I work. Fortunately, much can be done to improve the situation and restore a good night's sleep for the whole family. I will divide sleeping difficulties into two broad categories, with babies first, and then their older brothers and sisters.

Sleep problems in babies

Babies differ in how much sleep they need. Some may be satisfied with no more than ten hours in every twenty-four, while others may need as many as sixteen or eighteen hours. Many parents worry that some harm will result if their baby does not get a certain number of hours' sleep. In general, babies get as much sleep as they need, providing nothing is stopping them. Obviously, if a baby is hungry, thirsty, cold, upset or in pain, then this will need to be remedied. A change of diaper, a top-up feed, a bit of burping, a warm cuddle and a lullaby can work wonders.

Colic Many babies suffer from colic, which is a more severe form of wind. You will be able to recognize colic because your baby will tend to have bouts of screaming, most commonly in the evening; he will be in obvious distress, drawing his knees up to his stomach, and will be very difficult to comfort. Feeding sometimes temporarily relieves the problem. One of the differences between colic and more serious causes of stomach pain is that there is no vomiting or bowel disturbance, and between bouts your baby is perfectly well. It rarely keeps a baby awake all night, but comes in bouts.

Fortunately, the vast majority of babies with colic grow out of it by about the age of three months. I find the most helpful treatment for colic is a small amount of an anti-spasmodic drug known as dicyclomine. This relieves the spasm of colic and so takes away the pain. As the colic tends to begin at about the same time each evening, it is possible to give the medicine about half-an-hour before it usually starts, and so prevent it. In many countries this drug can be bought direct from a pharmacy. But, if necessary, your family doctor or paediatrician can prescribe it. Sedatives and painkillers are not as helpful for colic.

Different sleeping patterns You may have a baby who is perfectly healthy, contented and comfortable but who just doesn't seem to require as much sleep as you would wish. He may fail to settle in the evenings or wake frequently at night or even both. In my experience, such babies are usually lively and alert which may be some consolation to you and the many other parents who have suffered hours of sleeplessness. Incidentally, if anyone ever tells you that it is your mishandling that has caused your baby to sleep less than you would wish, you can firmly dismiss that as a myth for which there has never been any evidence.

What to do
I have found that the only way to cope with these short-sleep babies is simply to give in to them. Far better to organize your evenings around your baby than to hope that he will fit conveniently into your own plans. In any case it's a wish that is rarely fulfilled and leads to frustration, resentment and anger. Similarly, if your baby is restless at night and wants companionship, it's no use yelling at him and hoping he will go back to sleep. Certainly ignore the first whim-

per or two and hope he will settle down, for if every whimper is responded to he will come to expect attention. But if he clearly is awake and bawling for attention or physical contact, then that is what he should get. A baby frequently deprived of his needs (day or night) is unlikely to grow up happy and healthy.

Here is a 'straight-from-the-horse's-mouth' case that might prove interesting:

After spending a cold winter of sleepless nights sitting up with our first sleepless baby and trying unsuccessfully to settle him, my wife and I decided that rather than shiver by the bed of our second (when he developed the same pattern), we would simply take him into our bed. It must have been the consequent close, warm physical contact, that did the trick as he allowed us several more hours sleep than we had been getting with him. At the age of one year he settled readily in his own bed.

I know some doctors and psychologists express horror at the idea that a baby should be allowed to sleep in the parent's bed. This is somewhat surprising as there has never been any evidence to prove that it is harmful, and in many cultures across the world it is the normal thing to do. Usually, by the age of one, most such babies are able to settle and stay in their own beds.

If cuddling doesn't work
If all else fails, a small amount of sedative such as trimeprazine or promethazine may help – these are relatively harmless medicines, but they can sometimes make a baby irritable next day, so a drug-free approach is more advisable. Follow your doctor's advice on dosage and

length of time for taking the drug. Pacifiers and 'cuddlies' are harmless and may soothe your baby.

Sleeping problems in toddlers and older children

The nature of sleeping problems and the way they are handled changes as your child gets older. The first common difficulty in toddlers is that of helping them to settle. You may find that your toddler needs to have things done in a certain way before he can settle. This is a very natural and healthy reaction. It represents his way of gradually getting used to being alone.

The pre-sleep ritual

These before-sleep rituals may be very simple, such as your child wanting you to read a particular story. They may be slightly more complicated, such as his insisting you read the story sitting in a particular position and reading every single word. It is amazing how even very young children remember the finest details. You may find your child's rituals get very complicated and time-consuming. The purpose is in part his way of feeling secure and comfortable, but it also postpones the moment when you leave him alone. Providing you handle the situation calmly, being neither too intolerant nor too compliant but always reassuring, such rituals eventually disappear, usually by the age of three, though they can last for a year or two longer.

Fear of the dark is very common in childhood especially in the age group between two and six years old. It is best to be reassuring, and allow him a night light or hall or landing lights. Insisting that your child stays in the dark is most likely to make his fears worse.

'Cuddlies'

Nearly all young children become very attached to a special favourite object. This may be a doll, a piece of clothing, a small blanket or indeed anything that can be cuddled. These 'cuddlies' play a very important part at bedtime because they are a sort of substitute for you. It is worth encouraging your child in his attachment to his 'cuddly', for not only does it give him a sense of security at that moment, but it does help him to cope with learning to be apart from you. Needless to say, 'cuddlies' should never be removed as a punishment!

Refusal to settle

Some toddlers and older children refuse to settle whatever you do. Indeed, you might be involved in a scene familiar in many families when, just as you're settling down to a quiet evening, in comes your youngster who is supposed to be safely tucked up and asleep. Like many such children he may insist on staying with you, or repeatedly returning to the room you're in however many times he is put back to bed. To overcome such behaviour, you need to be firm and consistent. Having ensured that your toddler's basic needs have been sorted out, you should firmly insist on his return to bed. Any half-heartedness or inconsistency will be seized upon and used to his full advantage. 'Cuddlies' remain important and can be actively encouraged. Bed sides should be the only form of deterrent. There is no substitute for gentle but determined firmness.

Settling the older child

As your child gets older, any difficulty in settling becomes easier to handle. He can be encouraged to have some toys or books beside his bed, and it is not at all uncommon for children to have their own radios or cassette players. If he's sharing a room I think the rule should be made that radios and recorders should only be played if he's wearing earphones. You need to make the rule that he must not leave his room and that he must not disturb others. Again, firmness and consistency combined with allowing for the child's age and sleep requirements will usually lead to a satisfactory compromise.

Rewards

I often find that star charts or other rewards (see Chapters nine and ten) for the right behaviour are well worth using. You need not worry that rewards will create other problems. Many parents worry that they are bribing their child. This is not the case – bringing up children satisfactorily is based on all sorts of subtle rewards for doing what the parents want.

Night-waking in toddlers and older children

Between the ages of about one and three, many children will still wake frequently on most nights. Providing there is no obvious physical cause such as hunger, thirst, pain or other form of discomfort, it is best to remain as uninvolved as possible. If your child frequently calls for you it is wise to reassure him that you are near, but that you are not coming as it is night-time and you are trying to sleep. A repeated and firm statement to this effect usually does the trick.

Leaving them alone

Sometimes a child manages to get his parents into the position of having to be with him at night, for example, through illness. When he's better he still wants them to be there and protests bitterly when they try to leave him. Eventually everyone gets tired and irritable. As it isn't advisable for

older children to be in their parents' bed, it is best to help them get used to being alone at night. The best way of doing this is to encourage it gradually over a number of nights. At first, your child might be in his bed insisting on you holding or cuddling him. Ideally, you say firmly that he is to stay there, but you will sit beside him and hold his hand until he is asleep. Once he has got used to falling asleep holding your hand, you then say that you will stay in the room, but not hold his hand. You can, of course, talk or sing to him. After a few nights, most children learn to fall asleep with this reduced contact. You can then move yourself further away, until eventually you are out of his room. Your child gets used to falling asleep knowing you are just outside his room, and soon it becomes possible when he wakes for you to reassure him from your own bed. Each step requires your firm insistence that you are not going to allow any closer contact.

This technique requires a lot of patience, is time-consuming and tiring, but it does work, and it is better than being up all night, or getting furious and even violent.

If, when your child is older he still wakes occasionally at night, then, provided he is not too tired during the day, he is probably getting sufficient sleep. You should allow him to play with his toys, and look at books provided he does not disturb the rest of the family.

Worry

You may have a school-age child who wakes at night, or cannot settle to sleep because he is particularly worried about something. The best way of helping is to encourage him to talk about his worries, show that you understand and accept them, and then discuss possible solutions.

Your child might be worried about starting school, for instance. This might cause him to wake frequently at nights. Knowing he is about to start school and connecting it with the disturbed nights, you should talk to your child; perhaps take him to see the new school and meet his teacher. The chances are that his worries will quickly settle and he will sleep better. This sort of disturbance is a phase, which, if properly handled, should pass.

Nightmares
Most children have occasional nightmares, and unless they occur frequently (say once a week or more) need not be a cause for concern. If your child is having frequent or recurrent nightmares, he is probably very worried or upset about something, and you should do your best to help him tell you about it. Worries, once out in the open, are more likely to disappear than if kept bottled-up (see Chapter nine). There is no medical reason for nightmares, and the idea that cheese causes them is an 'old wives' tale'.

Night-terrors
Between 1 and 3 per cent of children between the ages of four and twelve are affected by night-terrors, which are different from nightmares. If your child has a nightmare, he usually wakes completely from it and can fully remember it. With night-terrors your child seems to be awake, for he is usually screaming or crying and obviously frightened. But, he is not arousable and when he finally wakes he cannot remember anything about it. Often he will be sweating and trembling.

Night-terrors are not fully understood, but unless accompanied by other disturbances, such as sleep-walking, do not mean that anything is seriously wrong. They invariably stop eventually, usually by the age of twelve.

What to do
Many doctors use a small dose of the tranquillizer diazepam at bedtime to prevent them. I have found that this is not necessary if you know approximately when the episode of night-terror is going to occur (this usually happens about the same time each night). The trick is to fully wake the child about thirty minutes before the usual time of the night-terror. In some way, this alters the sleep pattern and prevents the terror from occuring.

Sleep-talking
On its own, sleep-talking is common in childhood and is best completely ignored.

Sleep-walking
As well as sleep-talking a child may also sleep-walk. In fact, cases of sleep-walking are far less frequent (about 2 to 3 per cent of children of school-age), though more worrying. The main concern is not that there is something seriously wrong, but that the sleep-walker may harm himself. If your child walks in his sleep, it is important to make sure he is safe, by locking doors and windows, protecting staircases and removing objects he is likely to bump into or knock over. When sleep-walking happens only now and again, no treatment is required; but if your child sleep-walks often then the technique I described for night-terrors can be used. If this fails, your doctor will probably prescribe a tranquillizer such as diazepam, which may help. Sleep-walking usually stops by the age of fourteen.

No need to worry

Whatever sleep disturbances your child may have, be assured that they do resolve with time. However tired you may be, your baby must be your prime concern. Toddlers fortunately can be encouraged into reasonable bedtime behaviour and sleep patterns, and there are a number of ways you can help your older child to settle down, as we have already seen (page 23).

Toilet-training problems

It is strange that such an apparently natural business as toileting can give rise to so many difficulties, worries and battles. In this section I want to consider what can go wrong, why it does and what to do about it.

Toilet-training: when to start?

Occasionally, I meet parents who claim that their child was using the pot properly by the age of six months. Such a claim not only makes other parents wonder why their own child is so slow, but is also unlikely to be accurate.

Bladder control The earliest that most children are able to control their bladder while awake is around eighteen months, and while asleep twenty-four months. It is exceptional for a child to have any sort of bladder control before he is eighteen months old. Those parents who claim their child is toilet-trained earlier than that probably have a child who happens to use the pot when they sit him on it. If the child sits on the pot frequently enough, for example every two hours, it is perfectly possible that he will then give the impression that he has bladder control. Most children could be expected to be dry by day at twenty-four months and dry by night at thirty-six months.

Bowel control is usually gained between the ages of eighteen and thirty months. Before the age of eighteen months, most children have not developed the capacity to control bowel movements.

How to begin toilet-training

In helping children to develop bowel and bladder control, you need to recognize three necessary conditions which go together:

1. The child's body has to be sufficiently developed before he is capable of controlling himself.
2. He must want to please you by using the pot at the correct time.

Help to make pot-training an enjoyable activity.

3. He has to learn a way of expressing his readiness or need to use the pot.

Knowing the age at which control might develop (see opposite) should prevent you from pressurizing him too early. As long as you have a good relationship with your child, he is likely to value your praise and will want to please you. You can use that knowledge to promote successful training by encouraging him to use the pot once he has reached the right age and then praising him for doing so. Once he is used to using the pot when you encourage him to, he needs to learn the words to communicate his need to use it.

Why do problems arise?
If you do not wait until your child has reached the three stages listed above, you might be creating unnecessary problems. Pressurizing a child to use the pot before he is ready will make him anxious and upset. He is likely to refuse to co-operate even when he is ready. You are also likely to get worried and respond by putting more pressure on the child, who more stubbornly refuses. Soon you have what someone called 'the battle of the bowel'.

Even when he is using the pot when you want him to, he should receive plenty of praise for doing so, otherwise he may start withholding. Indeed, all children will withhold from time to time. There are many reasons for this: they may not be in the mood; they may not need to go; they may not want to please at that moment; or they may simply be asserting their individuality – a sort of children's lib!

What does your child make of it all?
Looked at from a child's point of view, the whole business must seem utterly absurd. 'There is my Mother producing a strange-looking object, taking off my diaper and plonking me on top of it; ow! it's cold. Now she's making all sorts of funny faces and noises. Ah, well, I'll give a squeeze if it will please her. Well, that seems to have done the trick. Hang on, why has she gone and flushed the whole lot down the toilet. Is that what she thinks of my efforts? Shan't bother next time!' Admittedly, no child of that age could think with that degree of sophistication, but he is likely to experience some of the feelings suggested.

Remember also that accidents are bound to occur – it is asking for trouble if you make a fuss about these. Similarly, from time to time children 'forget' to go as a way of getting at their parents. Children need to do such things, and it is best to take no notice.

Bed-wetting (nocturnal enuresis)
Most children usually learn to be dry by day at about two years old, and by night at about three. Nonetheless, nearly all children will have occasional accidents, and these should not be considered as anything but accidents.

What constitutes bed-wetting? If your child is regularly wetting his bed more than twice a week after his third birthday, then he may be said to be a bed-wetter. Anything less than this can be considered to be within normal limits.

How common is bed-wetting? At the age of four, about one in five children still regularly wet their beds. At the age of five, the number has dropped to one in ten, and by the age of ten, it is about one in twenty. Only one in a hundred still wet their beds by the time they are fifteen.

Why do children wet their beds?
There are many reasons:

1. Some children are slow developers. Bladder control involves complicated nerve pathways between the brain and bladder. These tend to develop completely by the end of the third year of life. However, it does take longer in some children. When that is the case, I usually find that other members of the family have been slow as well.

2. In other children, if they are undergoing any kind of stress at the time they are learning to control their bladder, then that is enough to upset the learning process. This is the same sort of thing that happens to adults who are temporarily unable to learn something because they are worried about something else.

3. Another group of children develop satisfactory night-time bladder control but then at a later date lose it. They may start bed-wetting again, either just occasionally or regularly. Those who only occasionally wet their bed do so because of an immediate worry, such as starting school or some other important event. Those children who wet their bed regularly after learning to control themselves are often described as 'regressed'. More often than not their behaviour is due to some major stress in their life. This may be to do with school or family.

4. Very rarely, children wet their beds because of some physical problem such as a urinary infection. Almost invariably if there

is a medical reason for bed-wetting there will be other symptoms of ill-health such as raised temperature.

What to do about toilet problems
If your child doesn't seem to understand what his pot-training is all about it is worth asking yourself the questions: am I expecting too much too soon? Am I getting too worried about it? Am I putting on too much pressure? If the answer is 'Yes', then you should stop; put the pot away for a while. How long depends on age. If your child has not yet reached the age when you could expect control (see page 26), then there is no point in re-starting until he has.

If, in contrast, he is within the right age-group, then it is best to leave off training for two or three weeks. In this case there is no harm in leaving the pot lying around so that he can show you if he wants to use it. When another attempt is made, make sure that you do not put any pressure on him. The occasion should be relaxed and enjoyable. Toys or 'cuddlies' should be readily available. If any distress is shown, quickly end the attempt, and try again later. The best time to attempt to use the pot is when you know his bowel or bladder are ready for emptying. Work out roughly when he is likely to produce, and get there first. When he does perform successfully, no amount of praise can be too much. Let him help with the emptying and flushing, so that he does not feel that his valuable gift has been mindlessly discarded. Remember, there will still be accidents from time to time.

If success still does not occur, leave a longer gap before you try again. It may well be that he is just not ready yet. Remember the age range for gaining control is very wide, and some children will not be ready until they are into their third year.

What if wetting persists after the third birthday?

First, it is necessary to distinguish between daytime wetting and bed-wetting.

Daytime wetting is less common than bed-wetting (even for those who sleep in the afternoons) and the two are handled differently, even though the causes may be the same. If your child is wetting during the day, there are a number of things you can do.

It is worth gently but firmly encouraging him to go to the toilet at regular intervals, hourly or two-hourly. In this way, he gets into the right habit, and also is more likely to remain dry. You should give him little rewards for being dry or using the toilet properly. Most daytime wetters respond well to this routine. Those who do not, and those who have other symptoms should be seen by the doctor (see below).

Bed-wetting at age three or four is still common, so you do not need to be too concerned. There are things you can do to help (see diagram overleaf). For instance, it is worth seeing that your child goes to the toilet before he settles down. You may find it helpful to ensure that he has no drinks in the hour or two before bedtime. You might also introduce some form of star charts. With a ruler and a few coloured pens make a large colourful chart in the form of a daily record. Every morning that his bed is dry, your child can place a sticky-backed star or other shape on the chart to show that he has been a success. Such a process acts as a reward and seems to encourage success. The diagram overleaf shows the different techniques and stages you can use if your child is wetting his bed.

Neither punishment nor scolding should ever be used.

If he is still not trained after his fifth birthday something a little more active may help. Still ensure that he doesn't drink too much before going to bed and keep the reward schemes. Try also waking him a couple of times and taking him to the toilet during the night – this may just be sufficient to stop the wetting. Your child's increased confidence from being dry will block out his anxiety and gradually he will learn complete night-time control. Occasional relapses are best ignored.

Should these suggestions not work, it is worth having a word about it to your doctor.

Regression

If your child has previously been dry at night and then starts bed-wetting, it is likely that he is worried or upset about something. It is worth talking to him about this and trying to find out what might be troubling him. I have found that the most common causes of upset are worries about school or school-work, relationships with friends, or difficulties in the family. If you suspect something is wrong at school then check with his teacher for any problems. At home it should be remembered that children are very sensitive to tensions. Parents often say to me 'But surely he's far too young to understand?' Certainly, your child may be too young to understand fully what is happening, but no child is too young to be upset. After all, babies are frequently upset without knowing or understanding what is upsetting them.

Any action you can take to relieve the stress may also relieve the bed-wetting. Again, remember that a sympathetic and reassuring approach is far more likely to work than being strict and threatening punishment.

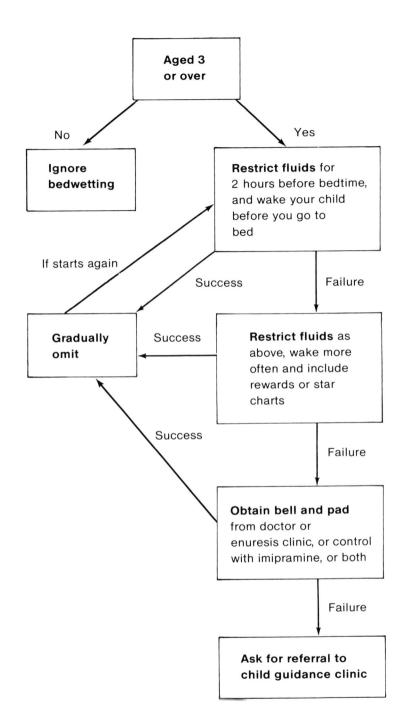

If your child is still bed-wetting by the age of three, try following this sequence of events to help cure the problem.

If, in spite of all your efforts you do not succeed, then you should discuss the problem with your doctor.

When to seek medical help?
You should seek help if:

- bed-wetting continues after your child's fifth birthday and despite your having used the techniques I've already mentioned above;
- there are other symptoms such as daytime wetting (if he's over the age of three), pain when he passes water, he's continually thirsty, faecal soiling, his appetite is poor or he's losing weight.

Your doctor will want to know about your child's earlier development, and other details of his health and his general behaviour. It will be handy for you to have this noted down beforehand. He will carry out a physical examination and may arrange some investigations such as testing your child's urine. He may also ask for a specialist's opinion. If he finds a physical cause for the problems, such as infection, he will treat it, probably with medicines. If he thinks your child is a slow developer he may offer advice. But mostly, though, he will be able to reassure you that time and patience will do the trick.

The bell and pad
There are a number of additional treatments available. The most useful is called the 'bell and pad', 'buzzer' or 'alarm'. It is a special blanket, connected to a small buzzer and is placed on top of your child's mattress and covered with the sheet. As soon as he starts bed-wetting, the buzzer goes off and wakes him up. The shock usually stops him passing any more urine than those first few drops. You can then rush him to the toilet. This helps him to learn to wake when his bladder is full and about to empty. If you can keep it up, the bell and pad usually works within three months, and you can then stop using it.

Other treatments
Some doctors prefer to prescribe a particular medicine for a short period. This is usually imipramine which has an effect on the bladder, though it is not known exactly what. This treatment is often best used with a reward scheme, and 'lifting', that is, waking your child and sending him to the toilet. Occasionally, doctors advise training a child to hold on longer during the day so that his bladder gets used to being fuller at night. Whatever happens, it is worth remembering that nearly all children stop wetting their beds eventually.

Disturbances of bowel habit

The most common disturbances of bowel habit are constipation, soiling and diarrhoea.

Constipation is a fairly common problem in childhood but it is more often due to psychological rather than physical factors.

There are many different reasons why children become constipated. These include poor diet, or anal fissures (a crack or split on the surface of the anus) or sometimes complicated neurological disorders. Poor diet is a far rarer cause of constipation than many people realize. Most of the children in developed countries receive adequate diets. Anal fissures are easily recognized because they cause considerable pain when bowel opening is attempted. Neurological disorders are usually obvious because the constipation

The bell and pad can be obtained from your doctor or a specialist clinic that helps to cure bed-wetting problems.

rapidly becomes severe, the child's stomach swells noticeably, and he will have bouts of vomiting.

Some children seem to have 'sluggish bowels' and are more liable to become constipated. On the whole, though, most children who develop constipation do so for behavioural or psychological reasons.

Psychological reasons for constipation Forceful or too-early attempts at toilet-training may well encourage your child to refuse co-operation. He will get into the habit of withholding and then become constipated. Once constipated, the bowel loses its elasticity and becomes sluggish, making the problem more difficult to cure.

Some children develop fears of the pot or toilet and refuse to sit on it. They then either soil their pants or

become constipated. Other children, while not fearful of the toilet, go through a phase of non-co-operation. If handled gently this usually disappears. If, however, a fuss is made, either as a result of anxiety or anger by the parents, the problem often gets worse.

Soiling (encopresis)

Most children have developed bowel control by the age of three. At the age of seven, about 1 to 2 per cent of children soil their pants. Soiling is usually a sign of more serious emotional problems. Very rarely is it due to disease. Occasionally it occurs with other problems such as bed-wetting, speech difficulties, clumsiness, and slow learning.

There are three types of soiling:

Primary soiling This includes children over the age of three who have never learned bowel control. Their faeces, which are perfectly normal, are passed into their pants. These children are usually not aware that they are soiling. They also usually lack bladder control, and wet themselves day and night. They frequently have other problems too.

Secondary soiling These are children of any age who have learned bowel control, but later seem to slide back and start soiling again. I see about ten such children each year. Sometimes they hide their faeces in places such as cupboards, or under the bed; occasionally they might even smear faeces on the wall or bed-linen. The faeces are of normal consistency.

These children almost always have a serious emotional disturbance. The only exception is if a child does this on one or two isolated occasions. It is possible that in such instances he is expressing some intense distress. If he can be helped to do this more directly (see Chapter nine), and the source of distress can be identified and alleviated, then the behaviour may stop.

Overflow incontinence or soiling If constipation is really severe, the bowel becomes partly blocked. Eventually, only fluid faeces can pass. This usually happens without the child having any control. It seems then as if he has become incontinent with diarrhoea. The danger here obviously is that the child might be treated for diarrhoea, which would make matters even worse.

Recurrent diarrhoea When most children have diarrhoea it doesn't last long and doesn't recur, and is due either to infections or the wrong foods. However, some children below the age of about seven do have bouts of diarrhoea from time to time, without any apparent cause. Despite the diarrhoea, these children thrive physically. One likely explanation is that stress is an important cause. Do seek your doctor's opinion if you think your child has this problem. Once you've relieved the stress, often combined with medicines, the diarrhoea should disappear.

What to do about disturbances in bowel habit
In the diagram on page 35 I show how you may be able to identify a child's particular bowel problem and how to handle it.

How to deal with constipation
If your child is constipated, there are a number of things you can do to help him. In the first place you should make sure he goes to the toilet regularly, and at least attempts to open his bowels. Try to do this twice daily at first. If he is frightened of sitting on the toilet, then give him some gentle reassurance and encouragement. Star charts or other kinds of rewards can be used. You can start by offering stars for simply sitting on the toilet. Once this is no longer a problem, give stars for successfully using the toilet.

Diet While poor diet is rarely a cause of constipation, a healthy diet can help. Fresh fruit or fruit juice, plenty of vegetables, and bran are all popular remedies.

Laxatives Unfortunately, many children with constipation are too constipated for the simple measures just outlined to be helpful alone. If this is the case with your child, laxatives may be needed for a few weeks. It is best to use those recommended by your doctor, and get his advice on when and how often to use them, rather than choosing one from a pharmacy. Sometimes, the constipation can become so severe that even laxatives don't relieve it, in which case it will be necessary to use suppositories or even possibly enemas. This kind of treatment should, of course, always be arranged through your doctor. Once the suppositories or enema have cleared things out, you will have to use a combination of all the above measures for a while.

As well as getting things sorted out physically, any anxieties or upsets also need to be sorted out. But remember, it is important to avoid getting involved in a battle. Firm, warm encouragement with plenty of praise for trying and for succeeding is the best recipe.

If these measures fail, your doctor will probably want to arrange for some tests such as X-rays, or other investigations of your child's bowel. Though unpleasant, these tests are not painful. If an anal fissure is found, this can usually be cured by the application of an ointment.

It is most likely that emotional problems are causing the constipation. Until these are sorted out, no amount of laxatives, special diets, or other treatment, will make a difference. Specialist help, as outlined in Chapter ten is required.

What to do about soiling?
Because soiling nearly always means some serious emotional upset, you must talk to your doctor about it, particularly if soiling continues beyond the age of three, or recurs after normal bowel control has been achieved. Your doctor will ask for full details and carry out a physical examination. He is also likely to arrange for some investigations.

Rarely will there be a physical cause, even if the soiling is due to constipation.

Specialist help is usually needed for other types of soiling. Specialists will probably advise you to use a toilet-training programme with rewards. In addition, they will need to look into areas of stress and upset in your child's life. They may want to do this with your child alone, or with you, or with the whole family (see Chapter ten).

Despite the seriousness of the problem, and its very upsetting nature, the long-term outlook is good. It invariably clears up eventually. With the right help, the accompanying emotional problems can also be relieved.

Worrying habits

Nearly all young children develop certain habits that worry, upset or irritate their parents. These include:

- thumb-sucking
- nail-biting
- teeth-grinding
- hair-pulling
- head-banging
- tics
- screaming and temper-tantrums
- breath-holding
- masturbation.

None of these alone means that your child is ill or seriously disturbed. If your child has more than one of these habits it may mean that he does have more worries than usual. If he has three or more at any one time (even if each on its own is only a mild habit), it is likely that he is indeed in some distress. Seriously disturbed children

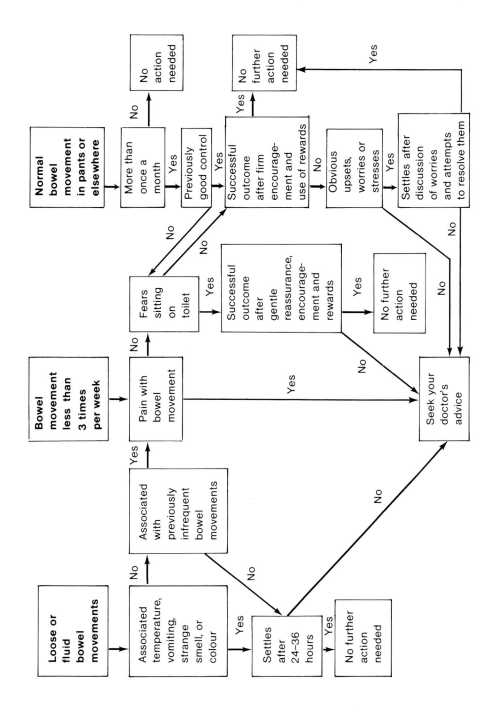

Use this flow diagram to help cure your child's constipation or irregular bowel habits. First identify your child's main symptom and start at one of the three top squares. Then follow the advice given at each stage, making a 'yes' or 'no' choice at each step.

are likely to have very definite behaviour problems, with or without habits. Some habits are more worrying than others, and need more careful consideration, but most of them need give no serious cause for concern. They are often more of a problem for you as a parent than for your child.

In this section, I shall briefly discuss the cause of such habits, consider how important they are, and at the end outline what you can do to help.

Habits are usually just ways of letting off steam (relieving tension) and getting comfort. We all have habits, whatever age we are. If, for example, you study a group of adults, you will find that at any one time at least half of them have something in their mouth, whether it be a finger, thumb, cigarette, pencil, and so on. Each is getting some comfort from the habit and possibly also reducing tension. Many habits in young children are so common, for example, thumb-sucking, that they can be considered as normal. Unless children are worried or upset by something or they get considerable attention as a result of the habit, the problem usually disappears after a while.

Thumb-sucking About one-third of all children suck their thumbs at some point in their lives. It usually starts in the second year of life and is a variation of the sucking that a baby is used to. When your baby sucks from a bottle or nipple he associates sucking with warmth, physical closeness and relief of hunger. Once the object of such good feelings is taken away he needs to find a substitute – commonly his thumb. Most children stop thumb-sucking by the age of four, and will have done themselves no harm. Beyond this age, thumb-sucking usually means your child has

a certain amount of tension or insecurity.

Nail-biting This is one of the most common of all habits and occurs at some time in about one-third of all children. Here we are considering compulsive nail-biting, rather than the occasional bite made to tidy up a nail. It is often just a passing habit of little significance. In some children, however, it lasts on into adolescence and occasionally even into adult-life. On its own, it does not suggest any severe emotional problem, but is rather a way of expressing tension, that eventually becomes habitual.

Teeth-grinding It is not very common for children to grind their teeth. The habit is usually related to tension. It occurs more commonly at night than during the day and although it is worrying to parents, it rarely means that there is any serious problem involved. It is usually short-lived and is best ignored.

Hair-pulling This is an uncommon habit which consists of the child twiddling, tugging or tearing out his hair. It happens only when the child is awake. It can be more serious than those already discussed, because if it is left unchecked for a long time, scalp infection can occur.

Children of any age from two upwards may pull out their hair, but the problem occurs most commonly in adolescence. In younger children it is usually a short-lived habit which tends to disappear if ignored. On the other hand, if the stresses which started it are not tackled, or if too much fuss is made about it, then the problem may continue. In older children and adolescents it may be harder to stop the habit, not least because the child may deny that he is doing it, and may be genuinely unaware of it. Despite its drastic nature, it doesn't necessarily mean that there is any serious emotional disturbance behind it, except in those rare instances when clumps of hair are pulled out and bald patches appear.

Head-banging This consists of the child repeatedly banging his head against some soft object such as a pillow. It occurs at some time in around 5 per cent of children during the first few years of life. Bouts of head-banging may occur every night and even several times a night, and can last up to half-an-hour. It most commonly happens while your child is awake, though he may also bang his head while he's asleep. Like other habits, head-banging seems to be a way of letting off steam and very rarely do head-bangers injure themselves.

Tics These are repeated movements, such as blinking, twitching, or shoulder–shrugging, which are sometimes called habit spasms. Mostly they involve the muscles of the face, head and neck. When the vocal muscles are involved, grunting or coughing occurs. Occasionally, other parts of the body are affected. The movements are rapid and brief, and the child has no control over them. About 5 per cent of children between the ages of four and twelve have tics. They occasionally last into their teens, and, rarely, into adult-life. Tics affect boys far more often than girls. Tics are nearly always a response to stress – again a form of letting off steam.

Screaming and temper-tantrums Bouts of screaming or temper-tantrums are very common during the second and third years of a child's life. They are simply a normal phase of development, and should be looked on as a healthy form of self-assertion. They may occur up to three or four times a day at their peak, and almost always happen when your child is frustrated or angry. In this respect, they are similar to breath-holding (see below). Your child will react to being frustrated in his attempt to do something by screaming or raging, hitting out, biting, scratching, jumping up and down, throwing himself on the floor, or hitting himself. Rarely does he do himself or anyone else any harm.

Providing these tantrums are ignored (as long as he isn't coming to any harm) they usually disappear within a few weeks, or at most six months. However, if your child gets his way as a result of his behaviour, then he will soon learn that when he wants something enough he simply has to put on a tantrum. In this way the problem becomes established and is quite difficult to get rid of.

Breath-holding This is one of the most frightening habits that any child can develop. Luckily, only about 1 to 2 per cent of children do this. They tend to fall into the age-range of one to four years old. What usually happens is that when the child is not allowed to do or have something he wants, he gets angry, finds he still cannot have his way, cries or screams and then holds his breath. The whole business may last for only ten to fifteen seconds after which he'll begin breathing normally again, or it can continue until he goes blue, and he may even pass out. Once he passes out he starts breathing normally again, and soon recovers consciousness. A certain amount of drowsiness is likely for half-an-hour or so afterwards. Unless fits occur (these are extremely rare in breath-holding), no harm comes to the child. If a fit does occur then you should seek advice from your doctor immediately.

Masturbation Children of all ages occasionally play with their genitals. This is a natural, perfectly normal activity. It's not the same as adult masturbation in that there is no sexual intent, and it is more of a self-comforting habit, just like pulling your ear-lobe or hugging yourself. What concerns many parents is that they think such behaviour is 'dirty'. It is important to understand that this is not the case. The stronger your reaction the more likely it is to become a problem. The best thing to do is either ignore it, or make a jokey comment such as 'Have you got something interesting down there?'. Threats to boys to 'chop it off', which used to be frequently made, will create anxiety and the need for more self-comforting habits. You need only be really concerned if your young child appears to be masturbating frequently and openly. If in doubt, discuss it with your doctor.

What to do about habits

Habits are usually a harmless response to worry or upset, or a way of letting off steam. They tend to disappear sooner or later. Whenever possible, it is best to ignore them while giving plenty of attention to the non-worrying side of your child's behaviour. Punishment or criticism nearly always increases the problem. It is sometimes helpful to offer your child a reward for short periods of time when he makes an effort to stop his habit.

If you find that your child's habits remain despite either ignoring them for several months or trying the rewards approach, then try to look into what sorts of things might be bothering him. Common worries for children include starting nursery or school, the birth of a brother or sister, or some difficulty in the family. Try very hard to understand what it is that worries him so that you can then help him talk about it and together you can start finding solutions. You may find that even when solutions are not readily available, talking is often sufficient to relieve the tension (see Chapter nine).

Whether or not the causes of worry can be identified, talked about and resolved, you can still make sure that you give your child plenty of comfort and attention.

Depending on the specific habit, there is usually a particular line of action, over and above the general measures mentioned, that you can try:

What to do about hair-pulling

If your child is a hair-puller, you can cut his hair quite short so that it is harder for him to grab pieces of hair to pull or twist. If the problem is really severe, you could get him to wear a bathing or shower cap at times when he would not be embarrassed by it, such as in bed at night.

What to do about tics

If your child has tics, it is important not to draw his or anyone else's attention to them. The more aware he is of them the more anxious he will become, and so have more tics. It is sometimes helpful to teach your child to find other ways of letting off steam, such as by physical activity.

If the tics become too troublesome, it is worth seeking your doctor's advice. He may prescribe some form of medicine that will reduce the tics. The most useful medicine for tics is haloperidol which is a form of tranquillizer. It is quite powerful and best used for short periods at a time. Doctors in North America, however, may prefer to prescribe a drug other than haloperidol. Your doctor may advise you to see a specialist who can offer various treatments including psychotherapy, family therapy, or behaviour therapy (see Chapter ten).

What to do about tantrums

Screaming and temper-tantrums are best ignored, but breath-holding that leads to passing out is sometimes too frightening to ignore. If your child breath-holds, it is well worth applying what is know as a counter–stimulus; for example, you could give him a slight slap on the back, or pour a little cold water over his head!

If, in spite of trying the various suggestions, your child persists in his habits to the point where you are yourself distressed by them, then you should ask your doctor for advice. He may be able to reassure you, or, alternatively, he may have some additional ideas. He may decide it is time to seek a specialist's opinion. There is a detailed discussion of the sorts of treatments the specialist may recommend in Chapter ten.

Aggressive behaviour

Young children frequently behave in an aggressive way, either just occasionally or in some cases much of the time. Occasional aggressive outbursts are all part of normal development. It is when their aggressiveness is persistent that it is abnormal. In the clinic where I work we see about thirty pre-school children a year whose aggressiveness has caused serious concern. Very often, the parents themselves can come up with the solution to the problem – or unknowingly add to it:

Alan, aged four, started biting his mother and younger brother when anything upset him. His alarmed parents responded by spanking him whenever this happened. The biting stopped but he became even more aggressive and started throwing things around and spitting. He also started wetting his bed.

Jason, also four, would sometimes hit his parents or younger two-

About one-third of all children suck their thumb.

year-old sister, especially when he couldn't get his own way. He had no other difficulties. His parents made it clear to him that while they did not mind his hitting them, they would not allow him to hit Joanne, and asked him to tell them what was upsetting him. They discovered that he thought they loved Joanne more than they loved him. After much reassurance the phase soon passed.

The different reactions of the two sets of parents have very different effects. If you can accept some aggression and think of it as an expression of distress, then you can talk to your child about it and help him find more appropriate ways of showing he is upset. Try not to respond with your own form of aggression because you are likely to aggravate the problem by teaching your child that aggression is permissible.

A problem common in this preschool age group and quite often found in aggressive children is that of overactivity. Because it is so common and because of the number of variations in behaviour, I consider it separately in the next chapter.

3. HYPERACTIVITY AND CLUMSINESS

Many children are described as hyperactive, others as clumsy, some as both. These children can be a great worry to their parents. In this chapter I consider the different levels of overactivity, and also consider the problems that can be caused by poor co-ordination, or clumsiness.

Hyperactivity

Children vary enormously in their level of activity. Some are calm, quiet, seemingly at peace with the world; others are just the opposite – 'always on the go', 'hardly stops for a moment'; most are somewhere between the two. Only a very small minority of extremely active children have anything wrong with them.

What is normal and what is not?

Most children have enormous amounts of energy. Indeed, it is surprising how active some children can be, despite the fact that they may not eat or sleep as much as you would like. Frequently, parents ask me if there is something wrong with their child who never seems to stop. In fact, it is one of the commonest worries of parents (about 30 per cent of parents have this fear), yet very rarely is there any disorder. It is simply the child's natural make-up, and such behaviour is particularly common amongst two- to five-year-olds. All you can do is envy his boundless energy.

There is one exception to the general rule that energetic children are normal children. About one in a thousand children in Britain (three in one hundred children in North-America) suffer from what is called hyperkinetic syndrome or hyperkinesis. These children are very excitable and overactive nearly all the time. In addition, they seem to act on the first thing that comes into their minds and are unable to pay attention to anything for more than a few seconds. They sleep for only short periods. As they can't pay attention, they have severe learning difficulties and such problems as swings of mood from high spirits to bad temper, slow development, convulsions, speech problems and clumsiness. It is hardly surprising that almost all such children have disturbed behaviour.

This condition is sometimes called 'attention deficit disorder', but in Britain and North America is it usually called hyperkinetic syndrome. Doctors have different definitions of these conditions, so do not be surprised if sometimes there is confusion about the terms used. What is most important is to know whether your child's overactivity is normal or abnormal.

How do you know whether your child's overactivity is abnormal?

The chances are very strongly in favour of your child's activity level being normal. You need only be con-

Overactivity	Hyperactivity (Hyperkinetic Syndrome or hyperkinesis)
Very active	Extremely active
Considerable energy	Endless energy
Can relax	Rarely able to relax
Can concentrate	Rarely able to concentrate
Not usually impulsive	Impulsive
Sleep pattern anything from poor to good	Sleep usually very poor
Mood usually stable	Mood can be very variable
Associated problems are rare	Associated problems include clumsiness, aggression, behaviour and learning problems

This table shows the subtle differences between overactive and hyperactive behaviour. Only between 1 and 8 per cent of children are diagnosed as hyperactive.

cerned if he (almost all truly hyperkinetic children are boys, incidentally) seems completely unable to stop moving – even long enough to watch television! He will seem to require little sleep and be quite unable to concentrate for more than a few moments at a time.

If your child is as overactive as this, then it is likely there is something wrong. Otherwise, his activity level is within normal limits. The table above shows the differences.

A problem or not a problem?

Brian, aged six, was always a very active child. He had been a poor sleeper as a baby, and even now, does not settle until late at night. He wakes at about seven o'clock in the morning. He is able to settle down to watch television, however, and to read books. He enjoys playing with his friends, but he always seems to prefer energetic activities. He is an even-tempered and affectionate boy, and happily settles for a cuddle.

Brian's record shows him as a perfectly healthy boy with enormous energy, but he does not show any of the danger signs of hyperactivity or hyperkinetic syndrome, unlike the next example.

Ben, aged seven, had always been exceedingly active. He slept very poorly as a baby, and even now can sleep only from about midnight to five in the morning. The rest of the day he is continuously on the go. The only time he keeps still is when building models with construction play bricks, when he can concentrate up to fifteen minutes at a time. The rest of the day he strides restlessly around the house, and is aggressive towards his parents and younger sister. He cannot sit down to meals, never watches television for more than three or four minutes and it totally unable to play with other children. His mood fluctuates between excitement and angry tearfulness.

Ben's behaviour is clearly worrying and he is undoubtedly suffering from hyperkinetic syndrome.

What causes the 'hyperkinetic syndrome'?

There seems to be no definite answer to this question. In at least half the children suffering from hyperkinetic syndrome there is evidence that a part of the brain is not working properly. Investigations often show that something has gone wrong during pregnancy or at birth. It is likely that this is the cause in most cases. Some doctors believe that food allergy plays a part. There has never been any proof of this, and it seems likely that allergy is relevant in only a small number of such children. There is also no evidene that lack of control or discipline by parents can cause such a severe problem. However, the way parents handle their child can influence progress, so I will discuss this in more detail below.

What about the associated problems?

The difficulties commonly associated with hyperactivity include slow development, learning difficulties, speech problems, clumsiness, and mood swings. So, if your child is very overactive, and has one or more of these difficulties, then you must face the fact that he could be suffering from hyperkinesis. If he has just one of these problems and is not overactive, then hyperkinesis is not the explanation; and you should look up the particular problem in the index.

What can be done to help?

Some 30 per cent of parents claim to have overactive children. Overactivity on its own is not abnormal, and does not signify a disorder or illness. You should not discourage your child's bounciness – be thankful, for it is an expression of health. The only problem is when it becomes a problem to you. If you find your child's excess energy hard to cope with, it is important to recognize that the answer does not lie in changing your child. Firstly, such efforts will not work; secondly, they are likely to upset and confuse him, and therefore aggravate the situation, and, thirdly, they will only add to your own frustration.

Much better is to be grateful for having a happy, healthy child. Take positive steps to try to find safe and acceptable outlets for his energy. For example, in good weather plenty of outdoor play and running around will help. If this isn't possible, then try organizing some indoors activity under your guidance. If there are any sports and other clubs nearby, they might offer a useful outlet for his energy.

What if your child might be hyperkinetic

If you are worried that your child is more than healthily overactive, and might be hyperkinetic, a different approach is necessary. In the first instance, it is worth checking out if he is as active at school as at home. If his excessive activity is confined to home alone, or school alone, then he is unlikely to be hyperkinetic. If in any doubt at all, then get your doctor's advice.

What will the doctor do?

Your doctor will want you to give him a detailed account of your child's development, so it is a good idea to have all the information noted down before you see him. This will probably start with pregnancy and delivery, and include all events in his early life. Tell your doctor about any illnesses, immunizations, injuries, and so on. He will carry out a physical examination. He may then offer you some advice on the best kind of treatment for your child, or arrange for some special investigations to be done. Many doctors would want to get a specialist's opinion and help.

What investigations might be done?

The most likely investigations are an X-ray of the skull and an electro-encephalogram (EEG). Both of these are harmless and painless to your child.

The X-ray can give clues about serious problems inside the skull, but it does not reveal much about lesser problems.

The EEG is a recording of the electrical activity in the brain, obtained by placing leads on the scalp. This may sound startling, but in fact everyone's brain has electrical activity, though at a considerably lower voltage than the sort of electricity we use in the home! When part of the brain is not working properly, there is a change in electrical activity which shows on the EEG. Hyperkinetic children often have abnormal EEG's but rarely do they have abnormal skull X-rays.

Brain scans are now also used in many centres. Again, these are harmless procedures. An injection is given in a vein, and some special X-ray type pictures are taken by a scanner. Any

A child having an EEG. This technique is both harmless and completely painless and measures the electrical activity in your child's brain.

abnormalities in the brain will be shown on the scan. In hyperkinetic syndrome, it is unlikely that any abnormalities in the brain will show.

Other tests Some doctors may also arrange for certain blood and urine tests to be done, but these are unlikely to show anything abnormal. A different sort of investigation that is very likely to be carried out is a psychological (or psychometric) assessment. These are often called IQ tests (Intelligence Quotients), though in fact they are far more than simply a measure of intelligence (see Chapter four). They can give clues to the presence or absence of anything abnormal in the way the brain works. Even if there are no abnormalities they can show in what ways children (and indeed adults) are having difficulties in learning and in using their abilities.

What treatment is available?

There is quite a lot we can do to help hyperkinetic children. I will divide the treatment into five different categories: medicines, diet, parental handling, school management and treatment of symptoms other than the hyperactivity.

Medicines

There are two main types of medicines available for hyperkinetic children. These can be broadly described as stimulants and tranquillizers.

Stimulants It seems very strange that stimulants should be used for children who are already very active. There is, however, a logical explanation. Among the very many complicated parts of the brain, there is an area concerned with arousal and activity, and another area concerned with rest. Normally, they balance each other. In the hyperkinetic child doctors believe that the area of the brain concerned with rest is under-functioning. The stimulants serve to make it function better, and so increase the body's ability to rest.

The stimulant most commonly used is methylphenidate. It can be very helpful to hyperkinesis but it can also be harmful. Therefore doctors prescribe it with caution, allowing only small doses, and for relatively brief periods. You can expect some side-effects, such as stomach aches, and stomach upsets. In the long-term, a child's growth can be delayed if the drug is used for more than a few months, but your doctor will be keeping a close eye on that.

Tranquillizers These slow down the part of the brain concerned with arousal and activity. The tranquillizers most commonly used are haloperidol, chlorpromazine and thioridazine. Again, they can be helpful but, like most drugs, you must stick carefully to the instructions given or they can be harmful. Doctors prescribe them with the same caution as stimulants. Side-effects you may notice are drowsiness, stiffness, abnormal movements and spasms.

Diet

There is no proof that diet has any part to play either in causing hyperkinesis or in its treatment. But, many doctors and others concerned with hyperkinetic children believe that at least some of these children are allergic to various foods and drinks. Additives, preservatives, artificial colourings and flavourings are some of the substances that are under suspicion in this respect. Some parents report that their children do seem to be worse with certain foods and better without them.

A caution There is no harm in having a sensible investigation into a possible food allergy. But do remember that in more than half of hyperkinetic children, there is clear evidence that the cause has nothing to do with allergy. Further, even if you do think the cause is allergy, don't leave out other channels of investigation or your child is likely to be deprived of treatment he badly needs. Far too often parents single-mindedly and desperately seek a food allergy, ignoring the doctor's advice and other obviously relevant factors.

Finally, diets that cut out everything that could possibly be allergic are restrictive, expensive and difficult to stick to. It is possible that by insisting that your child sticks rigidly to a dubiously helpful diet you might just create more problems than already exist.

Parental handling

Although hyperactivity isn't brought on by particular types of handling, changes in your handling can improve the situation. If your child is hyperkinetic, it is worth thinking carefully about how you handle him. It is important to give him a fairly structured day with plenty of activities. He will need toys to play with, though too many will distract him. He will need space to run around in. Remember that he cannot help being very active and distractable.

Punishment has little use in handling a hyperactive child. The only place for punishment is if there is continuing and wilful breaking of rules. The rules, however, have to be within your child's capacity. There is no point in saying he must keep still, for instance. In contrast, you can insist that he does not throw or break things, and that he does not kick, bite or smack people.

You should seek the help of a doctor or psychologist in this respect as he may be able to see ways in which you can change your handling.

There is no doubt that bringing up extremely active children is exhausting, frustrating and dispiriting. You will benefit from as much outside help as you can get.

School management

Your hyperkinetic child will almost certainly need to be in a school that knows how to handle such children. Very few teachers in normal schools know how best to help, nor do they have the time or resources. Hyperkinetic children need to be in schools where they can be in small groups so that they can get the necessary attention and control. These special schools arrange the school-day carefully to meet your child's needs.

Treatment of symptoms other than hyperactivity

All of the other problems of your hyperkinetic child will require special attention. Your doctor and a psychologist will advise you about any slow development (see Chapter four). Learning problems will require special teaching techniques (see Chapter four). Clumsiness is sometimes helped by physiotherapy (see opposite). Convulsions require treatment with special anticonvulsant medicines. If your child has a speech problem he will benefit from speech therapy (see page 56). It is best to try and put up with mood swings, unless they are particularly severe. If, however, the change from a depressed to an excited mood, or vice versa, is particularly frequent, or the depression or excitement is overwhelming, then additional medicines will be needed. The one most likely to be recommended is a medicine called lithium, which, if used correctly, can be very helpful.

What is the outlook for a hyperkinetic child?

This depends to some extent on how many problems he has. If he is extremely active and of normal intelligence with no other problems, he will slow down as he approaches his teens. By mid-adolescence he is unlikely to be very overactive. He may be restless and fidgety, but he should be able to cope well in most situations.

The more associated difficulties there are, the harder it is to predict the outcome. Obviously, each individual child varies, but even if there are many additional problems, the overactivity gets less with time. Fits can be controlled by anticonvulsant drugs. Clumsiness usually improves with age and physiotherapy. If he's a slow developer and has trouble with learning, these too will improve, but the amount of improvement is governed by how severe the problem is to start with.

The important points are:

- If your child is simply overactive, be grateful for a healthy child.
- If he genuinely cannot keep still for more than a few seconds, and finds it very difficult to concentrate on anything at all, seek medical advice.
- Although hyperkinetic syndrome is rare, there is plenty that can be done with specialist advice and treatment.

Clumsiness

Some hyperkinetic children are also clumsy but many children tend to be clumsy without being hyperkinetic or even overactive. They may frequently drop or break things and easily stumble or fall over. Some children are simply born clumsy. Others may acquire the problem as a result of difficulties either during pregnancy, (for example, toxaemia), or around the time of delivery (for example, forceps delivery), or following some accident or infection affecting the brain, such as head injury or encephalitis. While some children have a very mild degree of clumsiness, others may be 'all fingers and thumbs!'.

Other complications

Many clumsy children have other problems as well, such as speech difficulties, short-sight, and learning difficulties at school. Few clumsy children can write well, and most have poor or even illegible handwriting. They make poor sportsmen because of trouble with co-ordination between eyes, hands and feet.

Sadly, clumsy children get told off or teased because of their troubles. Needless to say, this only makes the problem worse by making them more anxious, and then more clumsy. If your child is clumsy, it is important to remember that it is neither his fault nor yours. It's not one of those problems where you can find the cause, and correct it but he can be helped considerably. He requires gentle encouragement for his efforts. Praise him for the things he does well. Physiotherapy may well benefit him, and your family doctor can arrange this.

Make sure that his teachers understand the problem and are sympathetic rather than critical. Make his life easier by buying clothes with zips rather than buttons, and shoes without laces. Take him slowly through the stages of buttoning and tying. Let him try them as exercises, practising them slowly and carefully. Seek your doctor's advice about short-sight, speech, reading and writing difficulties that are usually associated with clumsiness. Most children get over their clumsiness by the time they reach adult-life. The chances are that if your child is clumsy he will have some other talents that can be developed to make up for his clumsiness. I have chosen the following example because it illustrates many of the points we have been looking at:

At birth Ken was delivered by forceps. His parents noticed he was a little slow in walking and talking, though he was walking well by the age of two and a half. At the age of three he still had trouble saying certain sounds. They also noticed that he was short-sighted, and in particular that he was quite clumsy. He didn't seem to be able to use a spoon properly and would often drop his cup when trying to drink. He frequently fell over, and found dressing himself very difficult.

The paediatrician they consulted found nothing seriously wrong and explained to Ken's parents that these difficulties often came together. He was given glasses to wear, and started both speech therapy and physiotherapy.

Gradually both his speech and co-ordination improved. By the age of five he had overcome most of his speech difficulties, was no longer falling over, and could use a knife and fork. As buttoning up his clothes was still very hard, his parents bought clothes with zippers and Velcro-fastening shoes.

The key to Ken's improvement was really the loving care and concern of his parents who, together with specialist help and advice, were able to substantially help their child. In looking at the next group of childhood problems, those of slow or abnormal development, we'll see that the role of the caring parent is just as critical.

4. THE PROBLEMS OF SLOW OR ABNORMAL DEVELOPMENT

A common cause of concern for parents is when their child's development is delayed or abnormal. The child may also have accompanying emotional or behavioural problems. In many instances, it is possible to help your child catch up. In others, this may not be possible, but it is important to help him to get the best possible results from his situation. In all cases you need to be able to cope with what can be a stressful and upsetting problem.

In this chapter I shall describe the stages of normal development, discuss delayed and abnormal development and consider the causes and management of some of the difficulties that go with these problems.

What is normal?

The ages at which your child may smile, walk, or talk, develop good bowel control, learn to read, and so on, can vary a great deal. For example, he may be able to walk ten steps on his own at the age of eight months, or may not manage to do this till he is eighteen months. Either age is within the normal range. Very commonly children are slower than average in some areas of development and faster in others.

The first month
The very first thing most babies do is cry – which is both vital and natural as it is how they take their first breath. Crying is also important for babies because it is the only way they have of showing that they are upset. Indeed, in the first few weeks, healthy babies do little other than cry, feed and sleep. Babies are born floppy and it takes a while for them to develop sufficient strength to support themselves in any way. During the first couple of weeks of life most babies, when held upright with their feet touching a firm surface, appear to take steps forward. This is not walking at all, but a normal reflex action. Sadly, it does not mean that your baby is extremely advanced and the reflex usually disappears quite quickly as the baby matures.

The second month
During the second month of life a number of exciting things happen. Babies start smiling, a thrilling time for all parents, and also start cooing when happy, contented or excited. Around this time, many babies try to hold their heads up, although they manage this for only a few seconds.

Three to six months
Around the age of three months, babies show interest in the move-

Overleaf: Some of the stages you might expect to see in normal development of your child between the ages of one month and five years.

Cry; make running
movements with legs.

1 MONTH

Smile; coo; hold head up.

2 MONTHS

Show interest in mobiles,
rattles and people; enjoy company.

3–6 MONTHS

Sit up; roll over; put objects
in mouth; start babbling.

6–9 MONTHS

Crawl; stand up with help; make
first sounds; shy with strangers.

9–12 MONTHS

Stand unsupported;
wave 'bye-bye'; help with dressing
say few recognizable words.

12–18 MONTHS

Walk unaided; build 3-brick tower;
drink from beaker; scribble; use potty.

18–24 MONTHS

Run; jump; climb stairs;
feed with spoon; build
6-brick tower; say up to 50 words.

2 YEARS

Stand on one foot; ride
tricycle; use spoon and fork; copy
circle; build bigger towers; say up to
1000 words.

3 YEARS

Hop; skip; dress and undress
with help; more detailed drawing.

4 YEARS

Skip; ride bicycle; use knife
and fork; learn to read and
write; tell time; etc.

5 YEARS ONWARDS

ments of mobiles or of people around them. They also show obvious pleasure when played with or spoken to. They enjoy holding bright, noisy objects such as rattles.

Six to nine months
By six months, much more is happening. Many babies can stand when they're held, without sagging at the knee. They can also sit up and roll over. They will reach out for interesting objects and put them in their mouths. They start babbling, using such sounds as 'ga', 'ma', 'da'.

Nine to twelve months
Around nine months, many babies are crawling, and can stand up providing they're holding on to something. They look for things they have dropped, enjoy playing 'Peek-a-boo', and can repeat sounds such as 'ga-ga', 'ma-ma', 'da-da'. Most babies are shy with strangers at this age and are often worried by separation from people they know.

Twelve to eighteen months
By their first birthday, many children are able to stand unsupported and even take a few steps. They may deliberately drop toys and watch where they go. Waving 'bye-bye' becomes part of their repertoire as does co-operating with being dressed. They may now be using one or two words with meaning, such as 'Mama' or 'Dada'. However, such words tend to be used to describe everyone. Nonetheless, they can recognize and distinguish many different people.

Eighteen to twenty-four months
At eighteen months, most children can walk unaided and pick up toys from the floor without falling. They can build a tower with three bricks, enjoy putting smaller objects into larger ones, drink from a beaker using two hands, and scribble with a pencil. Many children at this age can use a potty. They show interest in other children, and play alongside but not with them.

Two-year-olds
By their second birthday, children can usually run, jump, climb stairs, feed themselves with a spoon, and build towers with six bricks. They use toys as if they are real objects, for example they might pretend to feed a teddy. Two-year olds are often dry and clean during the day, play with other children, and are less anxious about being separated from their parents. Vocabulary has increased during the year from one or two words to up to fifty. Some phrases may be used, for example, 'car go' or 'have that'.

Three-year-olds
Three-year-olds can momentarily stand on one foot, ride a tricycle, use a spoon and fork, copy a circle, and build even taller towers! Many children of three are dry at night, and with help can undress themselves. They are aware of whether they are a boy or girl, and what sex others are. A strong, natural and healthy interest is shown in their own bodies. They are much less anxious about leaving their parents. Their vocabulary will have increased enormously to around 1000 words.

Four-year-olds
Four-year-olds can hop, skip and may even be able to ride a bicycle with stabilizers. Most children at this age can dress and undress with help. Drawings become more detailed, and complex sentences and phrases are used. Thought-processes are maturing rapidly. First awareness dawns that there are other views of the

world than their own and that other people have needs.

Five-year-olds onward

Five-year-olds may be able to skip and to ride a bicycle without stabilizers. Their drawings are fairly recognizable. They use a knife and fork, not necessarily very skilfully. They are very sociable, interested in being with others. From here on, children become able to carry out increasingly complex tasks, and it is difficult to be exact about the average age for their achievements. For example, learning to read and doing simple arithmetic occurs between five and seven years old. Some five-year-olds can tell the time, while others may not manage that until they are eight. The concept of permanence (for example that when someone has died, it is forever) may be understood at five in some children, but not till eight or later in others.

Don't worry about variations

Remember that throughout infancy and childhood there is a wide age-range for the development of the various abilities. Most children are faster in some areas than others. For example, a child may be early learning to walk and slow learning to talk, or early in toilet-training but later in playing with others. I have quoted average ages. In the next section we will look at those children who appear to be slow in their development.

What is delayed development?

Most parents worry from time to time because they think that their child is falling behind in some aspect of his development. 'He hasn't start-ed walking yet', or 'she isn't toilet-trained' are commonly expressed worries. In reality there is a wide age-range for the development of skills such as bladder and bowel control, walking, speaking, learning to read, and so on. Inevitably, therefore, you will know children of the same age as your own child who have developed a particular skill before yours has. The other side of the coin is that your child will develop certain skills before other children you know. However, there are some children who are undoubtedly delayed in their development.

How may the slow developer be recognized?

The slow developer may be delayed in one or more of the following skills:

1. Movement
2. Co-ordination
3. Hearing and speech
4. Social behaviour.

It is possible that your child is behind in the development of some of these skills. For example, at the age of one he may be unable to stand up, or at the age of two he may not be able to use any words, or at the age of three he may be unable to control his bowels. If you are in any doubt about whether your child's development is delayed, you can check the normal age-range for the development of specific skills in the earlier part of this chapter. If, in consequence, you feel he is indeed behind, or you are still in doubt, you should discuss it with your family doctor.

Causes of slow development

We can think about slow development as being due to one or more of the following causes:

- Late developer
- Ill health
- Sensory problems
- Disorders of movement
- Problems of intelligence and learning
- Social difficulties

Late developer Something like 10 per cent of children are slow in their development without there being any obvious cause. Usually, such children develop most skills within the normal age-range, but are outside the range for one or two. A common example is the child who is slightly delayed in his walking and talking while being normal in other respects. This need not be considered a major problem, although undoubtedly it is a nuisance. It is possible that this is one of those things that runs in families. Such children usually catch up eventually, without it leading to any other problems.

Ill health If a young child goes through long periods of ill health, such as asthma or diabetes, or deafness due to constant ear infection, then he is more likely to fall behind in development. Once their ill health has been overcome, such children usually catch up eventually.

Sensory problems A child who is deaf or visually handicapped is bound to have difficulty keeping up with normal development. Unrecognized deafness may account for delay in talking. I will go into this later under speech and language problems (see page 56).

Poor sight or blindness, while more easily recognized, will affect the development of many skills, certainly until science comes up with new inventions that will help overcome the handicap.

Disorders of movement Occasionally, damage to a child's brain can occur during pregnancy or delivery, leading to weakness or paralysis of one or more limbs, or to other parts of the body such as the palate and voice-box. In consequence, development in movement or speech can be delayed. Sometimes, serious illnesses which can affect the brain, such as encephalitis (inflammation of the brain caused by infection or injury) or epilepsy, can have similar effects.

Problems of intelligence and learning Again, damage during pregnancy or delivery, or indeed after birth, can lead to deficits in intelligence and problems with learning. I discuss this in more detail later under mental handicap (see opposite) and learning difficulties (page 59).

Social difficulties It does happen, though rarely, that children are deprived of sufficient affection and attention to enable them to learn. All children need cuddling, loving, playing with, and being talked to, just as much as they need food and clothing.

Types of slow development
Having discussed briefly how slow development may arise and how it may be recognized, I want now to describe in more detail particular types of slow development, some of the problems that go with them, and ways in which you can help your child to cope with them. These are:

- Mental handicap
- Speech and language problems
- Learning difficulties.

Mental handicap (Mental retardation, education subnormality)

Children with mental handicap have a permanent and generalized delay in many areas of their development because their intelligence is impaired. Just how intelligent they are is usually expressed by their Intelligence Quotient (IQ). The normal range of IQ is between 80 and 120. Children with mental handicap have IQs below 70. About 2.5 per cent of all children have some kind of mental handicap. Those with an IQ between 50 and 70 are described as having a mild mental handicap, while those whose IQ is below 50 are severely handicapped. Sometimes their ability to move body and limbs is normal, but co-ordination, language and social skills are usually delayed. The diagram below shows the range of intelligence.

Intelligence is measured by the use of tests which give the IQ. There are various IQ tests available. The one most commonly used for children is the WISC(R) – Weschsler Intelligence Scale for Children (Revised). This measures such abilities as understanding, vocabulary, arithmetic, reasoning and memory.

Some causes of mental handicap

There are many possible causes of mental handicap. They can be divided broadly into inborn (inherited) and acquired. Among inborn causes are abnormalities of the chromosomes such as Down's syndrome (mongolism) or rare and complicated disorders of the body's chemistry. Occasionally, no cause can be found for inborn mental handicap.

Acquired mental handicap can

The IQ range over the whole population, showing the percentage of people in each range.

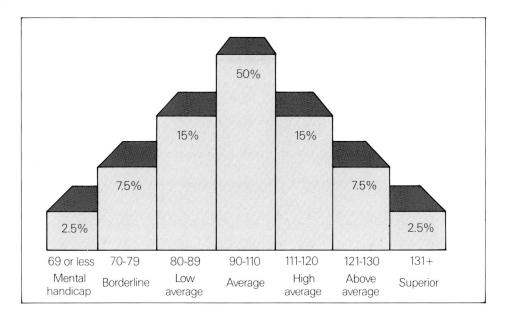

69 or less	70-79	80-89	90-110	111-120	121-130	131+
Mental handicap	Borderline	Low average	Average	High average	Above average	Superior

come about as a result of brain damage, which can occur:

1. During pregnancy, for example, if the mother catches a severe infection.
2. Around the time of delivery, for example, if there is serious bleeding from the mother, a traumatic forceps delivery or if the baby fails to breathe properly.
3. In the period immediately after birth or later, for example, trauma such as a head injury, infection such as encephalitis, or epilepsy.

What can be done?

Sadly, in most cases little can be done to overcome the problem itself, although much can be done to ensure that the child lives as full and happy a life as possible. Full medical investigation is necessary to assess just how handicapped your baby is. Some conditions require a particular kind of treatment. For example, epilepsy must be treated with anticonvulsant medicines while rare disorders of the body's chemistry such as phenylketonuria require a special diet. If this disorder is recognized and treated at birth, then it need not cause mental handicap. Problems that sometimes go with mental handicap, such as paralysis or language delay, need skilled attention to make sure that your child is able to make the most of his abilities.

Practical help

Psychologists will be able to advise you about how to handle your child's behaviour and what he will need in the way of education. Physiotherapists can help with any weakness of movement, and speech therapists can do much to develop speech. Where necessary, dietitians can give valuable advice about the best kinds of diet. Social workers can help with any practical or financial difficulties involved in looking after your handicapped child and are also skilled at helping parents cope with the inevitable strain. Do try if at all possible to get your mentally handicapped child to a specialized clinic and a special school where the necessary skill and expertise is available to ensure he fulfils his potential. There are many good state-run schools in Britain, Australia and Canada.

Speech and language problems

Speech is such an important part of human communication that any speech problems are bound to cause concern. For speech to develop we must be able to hear, to be in a satisfying emotional surrounding, and have people around us who talk. Babies normally babble by the age of nine months. Around the age of twelve months they start using single words such as Mama, Dada, cat and so on. A child of two, joins words together in phrases to convey ideas. By the age of three, sentences are used. As in other areas of a child's development, there is a wide age-range for speech to develop. However, if speech has not developed by the age of two or two-and-a-half then this is a serious matter which needs to be looked into urgently.

Delayed speech development

There are many possible reasons for delay in the development of speech:

- Late developers
- Deafness
- Defects of speech organs
- Mental handicap

- Aphasia
- Autism
- Deprived child.

Late developers Some children are simply slow in developing speech although there is nothing basically wrong. Just as some children are slower than others in learning to walk or develop bladder control, so some are slow in learning to speak. In the absence of any other abnormalities, slow development of speech is unlikely to be due to anything serious. However, if your child has not started babbling by the age of twelve months, or started some single words with meaning by eighteen months, it is important to seek a check up. Do not be satisfied with 'reassurance'. Insist on a full assessment including a hearing test.

Providing a normal child is spoken to frequently and hears plenty of speech, his own speech will develop eventually. If he spends a lot of his time in silence or is punished for his apparent lack of interest in speaking, then his speech will be delayed further. There are, however, a number of other problems that can contribute to delays in the development of speech.

Deafness As stated earlier, for speech to develop, a child must be able to hear. From the age of about six months babies start responding eagerly to new sounds. It is then obvious that they are able to hear. Even at a much earlier age, it is possible to gain a rough idea of whether your baby is able to hear. Young babies show a startled response to a sudden loud sound.

If a child's hearing is poor or absent, his speech is delayed. As he gets older, a deaf child will show increasing signs of frustration and bewilderment.

Deafness affects 1 in 500 children. There are many causes of deafness: some babies inherit deafness, while others become deaf as a result of infection or possibly medicines used during pregnancy. Occasionally, damage occurs during delivery. After birth, deafness can be brought about by using certain medicines, such as streptomycin, or from repeated infections.

'Glue ear' is probably the most common cause of deafness. This is a very common problem, often affecting up to 20 per cent of school-age children. It is caused by repeated infection in the ear and is easily recognized by discharge from the ear and often severe pain. A small operation usually relieves the problem.

If you have any doubts whatsoever about whether your child can hear properly it is essential that you seek help. Again, do not be satisfied with a 'He'll grow out of it', or 'Don't worry' – insist on a proper examination and hearing test. Many children who are deaf or partially deaf can be helped considerably in a variety of different ways. To some extent, the method used will depend on the cause of deafness. Hearing-aids can make an enormous difference. It is essential to start treatment as early as possible if satisfactory speech is to be developed.

Defects of speech organs Less than 1 per cent of children fail to talk because they have something wrong with their palate (roof of the mouth) or larynx (voice-box) or the nerve supply to these, so you can see that is quite rare. Disorders of this nature include cleft palate or cerebral palsy. In such situations, there are usually other problems too.

Mental handicap As mentioned

earlier, speech delay may be due to mental handicap (see page 55).

Aphasia (or dysphasia) Aphasia means literally 'without speech'. It is used to refer specifically to a group of disorders in which the child develops normally in every respect, except for the acquisition of speech. If there are any other problems of development, then this term does not apply. Occasionally, such disorders are referred to as 'specific developmental speech (or language) delay'. The cause is unknown.

If your child is developing normally in every way except that he doesn't speak, do insist on a very full assessment, as early treatment can make a substantial difference.

Autism This is a very rare disorder (1 in 2,500 children). Autistic children are late in developing speech, and have very odd speech patterns. For example, they mix up pronouns such as 'you' and 'I', and they repeat what is said to them. Usually they isolate themselves, not enjoying or seeking personal contact. They avoid eye-to-eye contact and physical contact. They enjoy repetitive play, often have repetitive habits, and may be overactive. The cause is not known.

If you think your child is autistic you must seek specialist help. This is best obtained from a child psychiatrist.

The deprived child Just as children require food and drink to survive, so they require love, affection, cuddling, stimulation and being talked to if they are to thrive. All of these are necessary if speech is to develop. The child who lacks affection, who is not played with and talked to may well not learn to talk. I see about half-a-dozen such children a year. It is very likely that there will be a wide range of other problems, including low intelligence and poor physical health and growth.

This is not the place to discuss how such situations arise. What is important is that once a child is recognized as deprived, early and skilled help from a child psychiatrist is required. With his help and by restoring the love, affection and care that has been missing, the deprived child can make considerable gains, even to the point of achieving normal development.

Stammering (or stuttering)
I include stammering in this section, for although this is not a delay in development of speech and language, some of the problems and treatments are similar. This involves frequent and involuntary repetitions of the same sounds. Mild stammering is common and affects 3 to 4 per cent of pre-school children as they learn to put words together. Providing it is ignored, it usually disappears. However, in about 1 per cent of school-age children, stammering persists.

What causes stammering?
It seems that the tendency to stammer is inherited. Once a stammer appears, the child's anxiety about it can inflame the problem. Similarly, the more fuss the parents make, the more the tendency to stammer can be aggravated.

What can be done to help?
In relatively mild cases it is best to ignore the stammer completely. If your child stammers, worrying though it is, do not try to make too much comment about it for this will increase your child's self-consciousness, and the resulting anxiety will not help.

If the stammer does seem quite severe, then the assistance of a speech therapist should be very helpful. She will make a full assessment of the problem and usually offer some treatment, involving teaching techniques to overcome the difficulty.

Your child can be taught what to do to help him relax, and to help him find ways around the blocks in speech.

What happens eventually?
Most stammerers overcome their difficulty by the time they reach their teens. A very few persist into adult life. Even so, as treatment techniques become more sophisticated, even life-long stammerers can learn to overcome the problem

Learning difficulties

If we exclude children who are mentally handicapped or who have delayed language development, there are still a number who, although of normal intelligence, have some form of learning difficulty. These are most commonly in learning to read, spell, write or do arithmetic. Approximately 10 per cent of the children have a learning difficulty. This does not mean they are lazy, stupid, or emotionally disturbed. We all have areas that we are good at, and others in which we totally lack skills. For example, I cannot draw however hard I try. Similarly, some children seem to have enormous difficulties in certain skills even though they may be very bright in general.

Dyslexia
The most familiar of these problems is dyslexia – difficulty with reading and writing. Dyslexic children may be very talented in many ways but struggle to learn to read and write. There are sometimes associated problems such as co-ordination difficulties, confusion over left and right, clumsiness and so on. The same applies for other learning difficulties.

Sadly, such problems are often not immediately recognized. The child with learning difficulties may fall behind at school, or develop emotional or behaviour problems before anyone realizes there is a problem

What should you do?
If you suspect your child has a learning problem ask for a psychological assessment, which will include an intelligence test and tests of reading and other abilities. This can be arranged through the school, or a child guidance clinic.

How is the problem overcome?
Children with learning difficulties need individual remedial help. Special teachers know how to help such children using particular techniques (see, for example, Dr Bevé Hornsby's *Overcoming Dyslexia*, also in the same series).

Associated emotional and behavioural problems
If your child has delayed or abnormal development, he is quite likely to have emotional problems as well. This is because he may be having trouble coping at school, or with friends, or indeed at home. It is even more difficult for him if he has an unrecognized problem, such as a learning difficulty. Under such circumstances he may well be doing his best to achieve, but failing, and no one knowing why.

His emotional problems can take any form at all. He may have aggressive outbursts, or be rude and defiant. Alternatively, he may become quiet, sullen and withdrawn. His sleep pattern might be disturbed or his appetite poor. Bed-wetting

59

may occur. These are examples of the possibilities, and virtually any of the behaviour problems mentioned in this book can occur.

What can you do to help?

You have an important part to play in helping your child, not only to overcome any behaviour problems, but also to fulfil his potential. But firstly you have to adjust your own expectations. It is hard to accept that your child has particular difficulties, especially if he is unlikely to outgrow them, for example, mental handicap. Whatever your child's problems you should not hesitate to discuss your concerns and reactions with other members of your family, and with the specialists who are advising you. It does help to get things off your chest.

A plan of action

So far as your child is concerned, you need to find the balance between encouraging him to fulfil his potential without expecting more than he can achieve. You need to know what he can manage and to praise him when he tries, even if he does not succeed. The last thing he needs is either bullying or criticizing.

Regardless of what type of delay he is experiencing, you still have to help him learn what is acceptable behaviour in and outside the family. He has to know what is right and wrong, what is safe, what is dangerous, and how to behave in different situations. Inappropriate behaviour should be discouraged and appropriate behaviour rewarded.

Eric, aged eight, had severe learning problems, particularly with reading, and he was also rather clumsy. When something went wrong or he felt thwarted or frustrated, he would scream and throw things across the room. His teacher noticed the same problems. A psychologist advised that less pressure be put on him to succeed at this stage, and that his tantrums should be ignored as much as possible. In contrast, however, he should be praised and encouraged for all the efforts he made even if he did not always succeed. After a few weeks his tantrums stopped.

Specific behaviour problems should be handled in the ways suggested elsewhere in this book, under the heading of the particular problem, or as discussed in Chapter nine where I give some general advice about parenting.

5. COMMON PROBLEMS IN SCHOOL-AGED CHILDREN

There are a number of problems that commonly occur in school-aged children. They can of course also affect younger and older children, just as the problems discussed in Chapters two, three and six can also affect children in this age-group. Many of the difficulties discussed may be short-lived, and little more than a part of normal development, just as temper-tantrums in two-year-olds and moodiness in early adolescence are normal features for these ages.

The various problems of the school-aged child can be grouped as follows:

- Worries and fears
- Unhappiness and depression
- Naughtiness
- Dishonesty
- School problems.

Worries and fears

Worry is a state of being troubled or concerned about something. It is a mild type of anxiety, which is an unpleasant state of tension.

Children in the classroom.

Fear is anxiety about a particular situation, and is usually quite appropriate, for example, fear of crossing a busy road. Worries, anxieties and fears are natural, normal and healthy. A fearless child is far more likely to injure himself. Common fears in the young schoolchild can include the dark, monsters, various animals, doctors, dentists, illness and death.

Phobias are extreme and often handicapping fears. The fear tends to be out of all proportion to the situation. Phobias can be handicapping because the child may try to completely avoid contact with the feared object or situation. For example, he may try never to go outside the house. Common phobias in school children include school, thunder, doctors, dentists and injections, and various animals and insects such as dogs or spiders.

Obsessions are persistent and worrying ideas; they often compel the child to take a particular action (compulsion). For example, many children pass through a normal phase of worrying that if they step on a certain part of a pavement they will be caught by a monster. They feel compelled to avoid that act. A more extreme form of obsession involves the child's urge to wash his hands for fear that something awful will happen if he does not. (Many parents would wish that their child suffered this particular obsession!).

Separation anxiety, the fear of being separated from a parent, (usually its mother) is normal in an eighteen-month-old toddler, but is clearly abnormal in a school aged child. About 5 per cent of children between the ages of five and eleven suffer from separation anxiety. These children tend to have a history of clinging. They become very fearful of separation at some point in their school lives, perhaps when they first start, or at around the time of changing to a new school. The anxiety may be expressed openly by fearful clinging and even screaming when they have to leave their parent – or the parent has to leave them. Sometimes anxiety is disguised as headaches or stomach aches. There may be an obvious reason why the problem has become worse, such as ill-health, or a problem in school, or in the family. At other times it is a complete mystery.

Shyness Many children are shy, to a greater or lesser extent. While it is quite normal in early life, it can be upsetting and handicapping if school-age children are too shy. About 5 per cent of school-age children suffer from marked shyness. Shy children are usually also anxious, but anxious children are not always shy. There is no single cause for shyness, which usually seems to be a sign of a particular type of personality. These children tend to lack confidence and have a poor view of themselves.

'Elective mutism' Some particularly shy and anxious children find it hard to talk in front of strangers. This problem, known as elective mutism, is very rare. It occurs between the ages of four and twelve. These children are generally very shy, anxious, timid and withdrawn. I often find that there are major problems for them at home or at school. They speak only in certain situations, usually at home, or with very close friends. At school or with strangers they are often completely silent, or they may perhaps speak in a whisper.

They are puzzling children because often when at home with their families they behave quite normally and seem fairly happy. The problem can arise suddenly, but more often it comes on gradually.

What is normal?
I want to stress that many of these school-age reactions are often normal. What distinguishes abnormal reaction is the intensity of the problem and to what extent it handicaps your child. To take extreme examples, if he is too shy to make friends, or he will not go out for fear of meeting a dog, or he is unable to go into school, or he washes his hands every hour or so because he fears germs, then he does have a problem. A child who continuously worries about many things is obviously suffering.

Why do these problems occur?
There is rarely a single cause for these problems. Children who have such troubles are often rather sensitive; they are worriers by nature, and frequently have close relatives with similar personalities. Unpleasant experiences are known to bring on these problems and threats can make them worse. Avoiding whatever it is that is frightening them may well make the situation worse.

> Karen, aged eleven was frightened of going out alone, travelling on buses or trains, and felt a compulsion to wash her hands every half-hour or so. She lived with her mother and grandmother, both of whom were great worriers. Her mother could not stay in alone, and her grandmother was terrified by a wide variety of noises. Karen was convinced that her father had died of a heart attack because she had not washed herself frequently enough.

What happens eventually?
Providing you are able to handle the situation correctly, most of these troubles eventually disappear. Shy or anxious children, however, often become shy or anxious adults. Providing the fears or shyness are not so severe that they make your child unhappy, there is no need to take action. If your child's anxious behaviour is causing you a great deal of concern, or if he is so overpowered by it that he cannot lead a normal life, then you will need to do something more than calmly attempting to reassure him.

What to do?
With all these troubles, the starting-point is calm reassurance. Your own gentle, sympathetic encouragement may provide your child with sufficient confidence to tackle and overcome troubling situations. Don't try to avoid the problem, as this often makes it worse. If, for example, your child is frightened of being away from you, then always being with you means he can never learn to cope with separation. The anxiety builds up over time and can eventually become crippling.

To avoid anxiety building up in children, I always advise parents to encourage their children to face up to the worrying situation. Providing you are calm, reassuring, encouraging and firm, your child may well learn to overcome the worst of the difficulties:

> Sally, aged nine, had always been terrified of going into school and flatly refused to go. Attempts made to get her there would result in screams, clinging, headaches, stomach aches and she would even vomit. Her parents tried every form of persuasion they could think of without success. I advised them that the only way they could

get her to school was to gently but firmly insist she went, and if necessary they would have to take her there against her will. They thought I was very cruel and unsympathetic, but having failed for four years, they eventually took my advice. Within three days Sally was settled in school as if there had never been a problem.

I know dozens of school-refusing children who have been treated in this way.

A similar technique can be used when children are handicapped by obsessions or compulsions.

Peter, aged eleven, washed himself every half-hour throughout the day, because he feared that germs would contaminate him. He could not go out, or mix with other children because of this anxiety. I advised his parents to stop him from washing himself so frequently, and simply allow him to wash his hands before meals, and after going to the toilet. If necessary, they were to restrain him. Very quickly indeed he lost the urge to wash, and one week later there was no problem left.

Another approach

Some worried children cannot be helped in such a simple way. If your child bombards you with worries to the point that you feel exhausted and furious, he is unlikely to stop just because you say so. A technique I find useful here is what I call 'the worry hour'.

Ten-year-old Jane was a persistent worrier. From the moment she woke up till last thing at night her parents received a barrage of anxious questions – 'What will happen if I can't sit next to Gillian?',

'What should I do if it rains?', 'How can I choose what to wear?' and so on. I suggested that Jane and her parents should choose a time that was convenient to them all, when they were unlikely to be interrupted. During this time, Jane was to talk about her worries as much as she wanted to, and no one should stop her. It was to be a time exclusively for worrying. In return, however, she would not be allowed to discuss her worries at any other time of day. If she tried she was to be firmly told that she must wait for 'worry hour'. For two weeks she used the time very fully, but gradually she found she only needed half-an-hour, and then a quarter-of-an-hour. After a month, Jane and her parents agreed it was no longer necessary.

This technique is very useful, and can be used again if the problem recurs.

Treating animal phobias

Children who are fearful of particular objects such as dogs, can be helped by being exposed to them gradually. One way of doing this involves introducing a very small and calm dog to the household. Your child gradually gets used to having a dog around and so loses his fear. I realize that it is not always possible or practical to have all sorts of animals in the house! What if your child has, for example, a horse phobia? Then you can help him by using pictures. Start by showing him a drawing of a very small horse, and then a slightly larger horse, and so on. Drawings can be replaced by photographs or pictures. After a few days you could take him to look at a horse, but from a long distance. Over a few more days, take him closer and closer, until finally he is no longer fearful and can actually stroke the horse.

Doctors and dentists

A similar technique can be used for children who are frightened of going to the doctor or dentist:

Luke was ten and could not bear the idea of having blood tests, injections, or his teeth examined. His parents came to me because he needed a dental check-up and also some immunizations. Firstly, he was taught to relax. This was done by asking him to tense up as many of his muscles as possible starting with his toes and working all the way up to his forehead. He then held them tense for ten seconds, relaxed them for ten seconds, and repeated the whole exercise twice more. Once he was really relaxed his father pretended he was the dentist and put a spoon in his mouth and 'examined' his teeth. The process was repeated and then a pencil was used as a pretend injection. He was soon ready to have his teeth examined and for injections and blood-tests.

There is an endless variation of such techniques for all sorts of fears and phobias.

Advice about shyness

Shyness and lack of confidence require a different kind of help. Firstly, never belittle your shy child, for this will make him worse. Praise any progress he makes and even reward him for it. Encourage very gradual contact with others. Invite a quiet child of his own age to your home, so allowing him to slowly get used to contact with others. Your shy child is bound to have strengths and skills and you should encourage these. For example, if he draws well, or can play a musical instrument, encourage this and boost his self-confidence by showing your admiration for his abilities.

When to seek help?

If your child's problems remain in spite of using some of the techniques I have suggested, or if he is handicapped by them or in so much distress that you are yourself very upset, then discuss the problem with your family doctor. The possible treatments are discussed in Chapter ten.

Unhappiness and depression

All children from time to time feel sad, unhappy or miserable, and crying is of course the normal response when children are distressed. As with so many other aspects of behaviour, what matters is not whether such features occur, but rather how often and how intensely.

If your child tells you or shows you frequently that he is sad or unhappy, or if he seems to be continuously miserable, or if he cries a good deal, then something is wrong. Depression to this degree, while not an illness in the way some adults are affected, is terribly distressing for everyone and must be taken seriously.

What causes these problems?

Occasionally, a child is miserable because he is unwell, or because he is in pain. It is usually fairly obvious that there is something physically wrong and your doctor can always check on this. Children sometimes get depressed after a virus infection, such as a severe dose of flu; but this only lasts for two to three weeks. If there is no physical cause for your child's behaviour, he is almost certainly reacting to something distressing in his life. This might be to do with school or home. He may be having difficulties with lessons, or a particular teacher, or he may be having trouble in making or keeping friends. He may be upset by tensions or problems in the family. There is always a reason for these problems:

Warren, aged seven, had been crying frequently for several months. He was often miserable, did not eat well and found it hard to get to sleep. His parents had spoken to his teacher who said he had recently behaved the same at school, but she was not aware that he was having any problems with school. When I met Warren with his parents, I discovered that they had been having marital difficulties during the last year, with many arguments. On one occasion his father had left home for a few days. Warren's unhappiness was an obvious reaction to his parents' troubles.

Parents often tell me that they are not getting on very well but that they keep this from their children. In fact, children are very sensitive to the atmosphere in the home. They don't need to be there while rows are going on to be affected by what is happening. Often, children's behaviour is an indicator of how happy or unhappy a home might be.

What should you do?

Naturally, you want to know what is wrong. It is important to check at school for any possible problems. You should also find a time when you can sit quietly with your child and try to help him tell you about what is upsetting him (see Chapter nine). If he does talk about certain worries, then accept them as being important, even if they seem relatively insignificant. Remember, what are small incidents to you can be gigantic to your child. For example, if he tells you his friend has stopped talking to him it is tempting simply to reassure him – 'there are lots of other boys and girls to make friends with' – but this is not always the answer. Help him to talk about his worries as much as he can, show him you understand them and sympathize with him. Then you can start solving the problem:

Bob was aged nine when he first became withdrawn and tearful, with episodes of sullenness and occasional bed-wetting. We eventually found out that he had thought it was his fault that his grandfather had had a serious illness. The reason for this, apparently, was that Bob had been rather difficult one day, and his grandfather had jokingly used the common phrase 'You'll be the death of me'. When his grandfather subsequently became ill Bob was convinced that it was his fault. Being a somewhat introverted lad, he had not been able to tell anyone. Once we helped him to talk about this with his mother who was able to explain the real cause of the illness, Bob rapidly improved.

If you are unsuccessful in finding a cause for your child's distress, or you are having difficulties overcoming it, do seek help from your doctor. It is important to find solutions, otherwise the problem can drag on and upset everyone. Incidentally, medicines have no part to play in these difficulties. For further ways of helping, see Chapter ten.

Naughtiness

Like so many other types of behaviour, naughtiness is to an extent just part of normal development. All children are at times naughty, often argumentative, and sometimes stubborn. It's the kind of behaviour you notice particularly around the age of two, and during early adolescence. At these ages, children are experiencing newly found independence and need to assert it. 'Why should I?' or 'I shan't' are familiar to all parents. In very young children, this is a mischievous testing of the rules – and your patience. A similar kind of exploration needs to occur in adolescence. You should not worry too much about such behaviour in these age-groups.

In children between the ages of five and adolescence, a certain amount of defiance and naughtiness is again quite normal. Usually it can be controlled. I see about thirty families a year in which the parents ask me for help because they cannot control their child: 'He is very wilful', 'He doesn't respond to discipline', 'He dawdles all the time and won't do as I tell him', 'He won't take 'No' for an answer'.

Finding the balance

Such behaviour is most common in children with stubborn personalities, and is often harder to overcome. These children tend to have parents with similar personalities and it's often a case of a battle of the wills. Then there are the parents who may be too lax, not offering sufficient controls for their child to learn what is acceptable. Parents need to be neither too controlling nor too permissive (see Chapter nine), as the parents of Sam and Jenny found out:

Sam, aged seven, was a terror. He would break crockery, pee on the carpet, hit his brother and sister, swear at his parents, argue continuously, and refuse to do as he was told. His parents had both been brought up by strict parents, and had decided that their children would have more freedom. Sadly, they had been too permissive. Only when they took my advice and started firmly, consistently and unitedly controlling Sam, did his behaviour improve.

Jenny was six when she was brought to me. She refused to do anything she was told. She would not co-operate with being washed, or dressed, and she always dawdled. Her parents tended to be rather controlling and did not allow her the kind of mischievousness that is usual at her age. When she was tired or unhappy they found it hard to make allowances. As they learned to be less restrictive, and to allow more messing about, Jenny herself relaxed and became more co-operative.

The answer lies in finding the right balance so that your child is allowed to test the limits, but is kept gently but firmly from going beyond them. Often, the parents' too-violent or too-soft reaction simply makes matters worse rather than resolves problems. For this reason, if your usual method of handling a situation is not working, instead of a double dose of the same, try doing something different, perhaps the opposite. Providing you manage to find the right balance, he should improve. If nothing you do makes any difference, seek advice (see also Chapter ten).

Dishonesty

Parents are often worried by their child's tendency to lie, make up stories, deny their involvement in some misdemeanour, and so on. This is not necessarily a problem, for all children do these things from time to time. It will become a problem, however, if your child's dishonesty becomes a habit.

Fantasizing You will need to be able to distinguish between fantasizing and deliberate lying. Fantasizing is something all children do – it is the childhood equivalent of day-dreaming, but often put into words or play. Fantasizing is a necessary and healthy part of normal development.

An extreme but still healthy version of fantasizing is the imaginary companion. Some children talk about a non-existent person as if he really exists – a companion who shares many activities, and becomes a good friend. Such companions appear on the scene around the age of three or four and usually fade away by the age of six. They may occasionally re-appear for short periods, especially during moments of stress. You need only be concerned if the imaginary friend is still around after the age of seven. This would then suggest that your child feels insecure, or lonely.

My own children, Gideon and Adam, when they were four and two, made friends with an imaginary person who had the name 'little bottle'. Often they would play games which involved him, and if one of them was worried or upset, 'little bottle' became a source of comfort. He was also a useful person to blame if something was spilt or broken!

Deliberate lying
Persistent lying, or deceitfulness, also suggests your child is unhappy, frightened or in some other way distressed. Try to find out what may be upsetting him and take action to deal with it (see Chapter nine). Remember, also, that it is possible that your child could be scared of the way you might react to him if he owns up to some naughtiness.

School problems

Children gain much more from school than education; they make friends (often life-long), they learn how to cope with others, and how to deal with stresses. For many children, school is an enjoyable and rewarding experience. Some, however, find some parts of school life stressful.

Anxious or shy children may find it hard separating from their parents, or mixing with others (see page 62). Children lacking confidence may become anxious that they will not succeed (see page 61). Others may not get on with particular teachers, or find certain, or even all lessons difficult.

In any of these situations, your child is likely to show his distress. The way in which he shows it depends on a number of factors, including his temperament, and your own responses. Because there are such a large number of reasons why your child can show signs of stress, you should always consider school as a possible cause of any problem your child has.

Underachievement
Many children fail to do as well at school as their parents hope, or as might be expected from their level of intelligence. Children who underachieve may do so for a number of different reasons. Some are unhappy, worried, or in some other way upset. When this happens, they are unable to concentrate fully on learning. Teachers often describe those children as 'lazy', 'not trying', 'fails to

concentrate', 'doesn't apply himself'. The answer lies in trying to spot and overcome the cause of distress, as we were able to do in Marianne's case:

> Marianne, aged ten, started doing badly at school in all her lessons. Her teacher said she was fidgety, distracted and often in 'a world of her own'. By talking it over with her, I found that she was very worried about her elderly grandmother, to whom she was very close, who had recently had to go into an old people's home. I encouraged her parents to explain what had happened and why, and they arranged for Marianne to visit her grandmother regularly. After a couple of visits, she seemed to relax and her schoolwork improved.

Specific learning difficulties
Another cause of underachievement is a specific learning difficulty (such as dyslexia) which I dealt with in Chapter four.

Simply describing your child as lazy or not trying, isn't going to help him much. There is always a reason for such behaviour, and it is important to find out what it is. If your child is underachieving, discuss it with his teacher, and try to think of any worries or upsets that may be getting in the way. If necessary, ask the school to arrange for intelligence testing. This can be done by an educational psychologist, or counsellor, either at the school or in a child guidance clinic.

Truancy
Truancy is a common problem in the age-range of eleven to sixteen, and is a big temptation to underachievers. I shall be discussing truancy along with other problems of that age-group in the next chapter.

6. ADOLESCENT PROBLEMS

Adolescence is that time between the onset of puberty (eleven to fourteen) and the age of eighteen or so –the time of transition from childhood to adulthood. It is almost always a time of some difficulty for both the teenager and his parents. There are a number of reasons for this:

1. The teenager is beginning to assert his independence and his right to his own opinions. Inevitably, this can create tensions and arguments, and can distance him from his family.

2. He is far more readily influenced by his friends than is the younger child. This means that your own influence lessens. The teenager adopts different, and sometimes opposing attitudes and interests to those of the family. Common examples include the latest (and often to his parents, outrageous) fashions in clothes, hairstyle or music.

3. The teenager experiences quite dramatic physical changes, both in terms of growth and sexuality. Emerging sexual

Young punks.

feelings can be frightening, confusing and the source of guilt and frustration.

4. Adolescents can become extremely self-conscious and this, along with their generally heightened emotions, can make it difficult for parents to advise and reassure.

Fortunately, most teenagers survive adolescence without too much trauma. If anything, it is the parents who are likely to suffer most. Nonetheless, there are a number of difficulties adolescents can experience, some of which, however tiresome to themselves and their parents, are really normal aspects of this stage, while others are clearly abnormal and must be handled as promptly as possible.

Mood variations

Probably the most common worry to parents is their teenager's moodiness. He may at times be very quiet, sullen and withdrawn: 'He gets so moody'. At other times he may be just the opposite – boisterous, excited, confident. On some days he may be totally insensitive to your own needs, and on others just the opposite. This unpredictability and extreme variability is not abnormal. It need only be a cause of proper concern if your child is also getting into trouble, failing to cope at school or is having difficulty in his relationships with others of his own age.

Sexual curiosity and experimentation

This is another common feature of adolescence. Sexual curiosity and arousal are normal and healthy. Remember also that interest in one's own sex is also a normal feature of early adolescent development. Sexual curiosity and arousal invariably lead to some form of sexual behaviour.

Masturbation is the most common form of sexual behaviour in early adolescence. Contrary to previously held views, masturbation causes no harm whatsoever. Indeed, it is a necessary outlet for considerable sexual energy in an age-group where sexual intercourse is neither necessarily available nor appropriate.

Interest in the opposite sex soon develops in most adolescents as a strong, healthy and normal stage in their growing up. Attitudes towards sexual relationships in adolescence vary in different cultures. In most developed countries such relationships are frowned upon, both legally and morally, below the age of sixteen. Whatever age is considered suitable for sexual activity to start is arbitrary because adolescents develop both emotionally and physically at different rates. Some adolescents are mature enough to cope by the age of fifteen, others are not ready till they are very much older.

Promiscuity, that is indiscriminate sexual relationships with no emotional attachments, is likely to be a response to a sense of loneliness or worthlessness. Promiscuous behaviour is an attempt to gain affection, attention and some self-esteem. Generally it has the opposite effect.

Homosexual relationships are not at all unusual or abnormal during early adolescence. The combination of sexual arousal and need for emotional involvement with people of their own age outside the family can lead to homosexual activity. However awful this may seem to you, it is not uncommon and there is no evidence that it is in any way harmful.

Not all these relationships are physical, however, and it is quite normal to develop intense 'crushes' on particularly attractive or popular members of the same sex. In the vast majority of young people this kind of activity is rapidly replaced by interest in the opposite sex.

True homosexuality, that is, a physical interest in the same sex that carries on into adulthood is not caused by homosexual experimentation in early adolescence. Its roots lie in a combination of hormonal influences and bad relationships with parents in early life. Attitudes have changed to the point where it cannot be said that homosexuality is a disorder. What is more significant here is whether or not the homosexual is happy with his (or her) sexuality. Adolescents are likely to be confused and worried by a homosexual tendency. Even in adult-life, many homosexuals have difficulty in adjusting to being 'different'.

Depression and self-damaging behaviour

I referred earlier to moodiness. All teenagers have spells of moodiness, seeming to be unhappy and irritable. However, some suffer a more serious problem, that of depression, which in adolescence is not uncommon. The effects of depression are that the child becomes persistently unhappy, he sleeps and eats poorly, cannot concentrate, tends to be listless and tearful and does poorly at school. He may also be irritable, and complain of physical symptoms such as stomach aches, headache, sickness or feeling faint.

Danger point Some teenagers become so depressed that they may harm themselves, either as a way of trying to get help, or even in a genuine attempt to kill themselves. Only a few teenagers actually kill themselves, but many harm themselves. The most common forms of self-harm are taking an overdose of tablets, or scratching or cutting wrists. Although this kind of behaviour is often carried out in such a way that no serious harm can occur, it is always a sign of intense distress and you should take it seriously.

The cause of depression is often not clear. It may be due to family tensions, or difficulties at school, or in relationships with others. Occasionally, even after lengthy efforts to find out what is going wrong, nothing is discovered. But whether there is an obvious cause or not, you should always seek help if your teenager is attempting to harm himself.

Truancy

This differs from school-refusal or school-phobia (see Chapter five). Unlike school-refusers, truants are neither fearful of school nor of separating from their parents. Often they say they are going to school, but fail to turn up, or they go to school to register, and then leave. They prefer to be out with friends, and often, for lack of something to do, they roam around and get themselves into trouble.

Adolescents may play truant because they are bored or fed up with school, or because their friends play truant. Some fail to turn up because they find the work too hard for them, particularly if they are unrecognized slow-developers (see page 49). Occasionally, parents encourage truancy by not being insistent enough about school attendance.

Truancy, which is both common and widespread in many poor, inner-city areas, is a cause for concern not only because such children are breaking the law, and not getting an education, but also because they are likely to get into other types of trouble. If your child is truanting, you must take a firm line and insist he attends regularly. If you are unsuccessful, seek help (see Chapter ten).

Antisocial behaviour

Bullying, stealing, persistent lying, cruelty and aggression, are among some of the problems that might cause you considerable concern. This kind of behaviour is known to occur much more often in cities and towns than in country areas. There are many causes and they are liable to vary in different cultures. In general, however, some of the more important causes of antisocial behaviour include the bad influence of some friends, and the wrong kind of parental discipline, especially where it is either too harsh or too soft – and on occasion, non-existent. Some people think that excessive exposure to films portraying such behaviour may also contribute. You should take seriously any form of antisocial behaviour.

Darren was aged fourteen when I saw him. He had apparently always been an adventurous and boisterous lad, but had started mixing at school with a group who occasionally played truant, stayed out late at night and made a nuisance of themselves wherever they went. His mother adored him and thought it was part and parcel of growing up, having seen her own brothers behave in this way. His father, who had had a very strict upbringing, took the opposite view, and on more than one occasion had hit him when he found out about his truancy. His parents were unable to agree on a joint course of action so he largely ignored them. Darren increasingly

enjoyed being with his friends, and he got into more trouble. Eventually, he was caught trying to break into a parking-meter, and was fined by the Court. Unfortunately, his parents were still unable to work together, and Darren went on to develop delinquent behaviour.

Drug experimentation and abuse

Tragically, this is becoming an increasingly common problem in many cultures. Most teenagers experiment at some time. This is most commonly with cigarettes or alcohol, though glue-sniffing and smoking marijuana are also very popular. Many adolescents are persuaded to try what are known as hard drugs, such as morphine and heroin.

Bad influences

The biggest cause of drug-abuse is the influence of others. If parents smoke or drink, it is highly likely that their children will. If friends experiment with drugs then it is quite hard to resist the pressure to join in. The attitudes of close relatives or friends is very influential. If you smoke, do not be surprised if your child smokes – or experiments with other drugs.

Experimentation can soon become addiction

Drug experimentation is a desperately serious matter for a variety of reasons. All drugs are physically harmful, and most are addictive. Serious ill-health and death from drug-abuse has recently reached epidemic proportions.

If your child is using drugs or alcohol, you should be able to recognize the fact by a fairly drastic personality change, markedly unpredictable behaviour, excess sleepiness, loss of skills or failure at school.

Physical ill health is common. If injections are being used, needle-marks can often be found, usually in the arms.

> Simon, aged fifteen, had always been a bright and happy lad. Over a period of six months he became extremely moody, withdrawn and irritable. He was unpleasant to his family and unco-operative. He lost interest in his appearance, started doing badly at school, and refused to get up in the mornings. Alerted to the possibility of drug addiction, his parents searched his clothes and room and eventually found discarded tubes of glue in the waste basket.

If you are the slightest bit concerned that your child is using drugs, speak to him about it, try to help him see that he will harm himself and per-suade him to go with you to talk it over with the doctor. If you want to ensure your teenager does not abuse drugs, you must make sure you are setting the right example, and that he is well-informed about the appall-ing dangers.

Psychosis

About 1 in 200 adolescents can suffer from severe mental illnesses usually grouped under the heading of psy-chosis. The form of psychosis that most people have heard of is schizophrenia. In a psychotic illness, such as schizophrenia, there is a dramatic and severe disturbance of behaviour. It may happen suddenly or be gradual. There is usually a change in the young person's mood, and in his level of activity – either lethargic or hyperactive – while generally his behaviour may be out-rageous. His thoughts will be often very confused and rambling, and may be slowed down or speeded up. He usually loses his inhibitions. Schizo-phrenics often hear voices and have delusions-convictions that they are someone else, or that something is happening even though it is obviously untrue. Sooner or later it becomes obvious that something is seriously wrong and that it isn't going to get better without medical help.

How and why

Psychotic illnesses may arise out of the blue, though there is sometimes someone else in the wider family who has also suffered from them. They are known to be brought on by drug-abuse, and occasionally they are a response to severe stress:

> Stuart was fourteen and had always been a kind and cheerful boy, des-pite losing a brother from cancer seven years earlier, when his brother was also fourteen. In the space of one year his mother died, and his elder sister married and left home. Stuart's teacher noticed that he was behaving oddly in the classroom and that he was not con-centrating on his work. At home, he lost his appetite and interest in his surroundings. He would sit for hours staring into space. Occasion-ally he would suddenly swear at his father, or throw something at him. Eventually he completely stopped eating and drinking. On admission to hospital he was found to be suf-fering from schizophrenia.

Stuart's illness was undoubtedly a response to the very severe stresses of recent months. His sister had also had an episode of schizophrenia so it was likely that it was in part gen-etically influenced. Fortunately, with the right medication and some family and individual psychotherapy (see Chapter ten), he recovered.

If your child's behaviour changes

in a dramatic way and becomes very worrying, you must consider the possibility of a psychotic illness (or of drug-abuse, see page 73), and you should urgently seek your doctor's advice.

What should you do if you are worried about your teenager?

The first step is to ask yourself whether the behaviour you are worried about is the sort of behaviour that normally occurs in adolescence. Examples of this include moodiness, argumentativeness, and preferring to be alone or with friends, rather than with you. Your teenager needs to show he is different from you. He does this by adopting current fashions in clothes, hairstyle, music and so on. He wants to be more independent and to stay out late. All this is quite normal, and so long as his behaviour is harmless you need not be concerned. Occasionally, you may have to take a deep breath, or count to ten, or walk out of the room. Adolescent behaviour can be infuriating, but providing no harm is done, it should not always be challenged. Setting the limits is important, but the limits should be wide enough to allow for healthy exploration.

Setting limits and keeping them

If your teenager is exceeding the limits, or getting into trouble, then you must put your foot down. This is important; the line has to be drawn somewhere and you must be seen to be in charge. You may decide it is reasonable for him to stay out until, for example, 11 p.m. but not beyond. If he persistently defies you then you may need to insist on an earlier time home, or even staying in a few times when he wants to go out. You may be able to accept sullenness and moodi-

ness, but if he is frequently rude, you may have to demand an improvement.

Peter, aged fifteen, had over the previous year become increasingly difficult. He would argue against anything his parents said. He was aggressive to his younger brother and sister, and had started getting into trouble at school. His parents were bewildered by this change in personality from a previously friendly and easy-going lad. Initially, they allowed him free-rein on the basis that he had never been a problem before, and they had not had to be unduly strict with him. Eventually, his school teacher asked them in for a chat about him, and suggested that they be far firmer with him. There was an immediate improvement. When John, his thirteen-year-old brother, started copying him, they were able to allow a certain amount of self-assertiveness, but applied limits far sooner so that John's behaviour never became a cause for concern.

- If your teenager's behaviour is harmful or beyond what you might normally expect, the next step is to try to understand what is going wrong.
- Depression and self-harming behaviour are almost always responses to stresses with which he cannot cope.
- Adolescents whose behaviour is antisocial or who play truant are often copying friends, and responding to either laxness or over-control by parents.
- Drug-abusers are usually responding both to stresses and copying others. Sexual problems are most often a reflection of deeper difficulties in coping with growing-up.

What can you do?

You should ask yourself a number of questions:

1. Am I allowing sufficient independence, but setting appropriate limits?
2. Am I understanding the sorts of stresses my child might be experiencing? For example, coping with the opposite sex, school pressures, and so on?
3. Am I helping him to talk about things that might be bothering him? For example, concerns about getting a job.
4. Are there tensions in the family that might be upsetting him even though he is not directly involved in them?
5. Do I know how things are at school?

Janice, aged sixteen, had been rather quiet in the last few weeks, and had not been eating or sleeping as well as usual. Seemingly out of the blue she swallowed twelve aspirins, and left a note saying she was so miserable she wanted to die. Fortunately, her elder sister found her, and she was taken to hospital in time to prevent serious harm occuring. Later, she told me that she was upset by the tensions at home, and frightened that her parents might separate. She was also worried that she might not find a job when she left school. Her parents expressed surprise that she knew anything of their own problems and said that she had not told them about her fears of unemployment. We agreed that the whole family should in future talk openly with each other about their various problems. Janice fortunately recovered fully, in part at least because her parents helped her to cope with her own worries.

Teenage sex

Masturbation and wet dreams are normal in teenage boys, and it is sad that they so often feel ashamed and guilty.

Julian, aged thirteen, became very secretive and begged his mother not to go into his room. She wondered if he was messing about with drugs and became quite worried. She explored his room while he was at school, and discovered nothing more than slightly damp and stained bedsheets.

Incidentally, parents sometimes ask what they should do if they walk into their child's room and find him involved in sexual activity. Firstly, I suggest that a decision has to be made about whether you have the right to walk in without first knocking. Everyone needs privacy. It is probably best to apologize for intruding. Secondly, you have to decide on your attitude to your teenagers' sexual behaviour. Masturbation is so normal it can safely be ignored. But with regard to heavy petting or sexual intercourse, some parents allow this in their home; others would be horrified. What is most important is that teenagers behave responsibly, both physically and emotionally. This is too much to ask of some but not all teenagers. We are living in an age of relative sexual freedom, and parental disapproval will not necessarily stop this. In the long run it will be far better to make sure of your child's responsible behaviour by seeing to it that he is fully informed about sexual matters and about his attitude and conduct towards others.

When your solutions aren't enough

If, having answered all the questions posed above and taken appropriate action you are still worried about your teenager's behaviour, then be firm and insist that he seeks help, preferably with you there, but on his own if necessary. Your doctor should be able to help you, either with advice or reassurance. He may, however, suggest the need for more specialized help. You should take his advice on such matters. Adolescent troubles do frequently settle in time. But if your doctor remains concerned, then it is important to get additional help.

7. PSYCHOSOMATIC PROBLEMS

More nonsense is spoken and written about psychosomatic illness then virtually any other type of medical problem. The word 'psychosomatic' means mind and body. It is best used to describe a situation in which the mind and body combine to produce physical symptoms. A common example of this is a 'tension headache'. Anxiety or worry, which are states of mind, produce spasm of the muscles in your scalp, which you are aware of as a headache. Many common bodily reactions are psychosomatic. For example, crying; unhappiness (an emotion) produces tears (a physical reaction); or fear (an emotion) produces palpitations (a physical reaction). Such reactions like these are happening much of the time in everyone regardless of age. So there is nothing to be ashamed of, or surprised about, when one of your bodily reactions is described as psychosomatic.

What do they mean?

Many aches and pains and other physical symptoms are known to arise from our state of mind, exercising a powerful influence on our body, for example, headaches, stomach aches, limb pains, vomiting, diarrhoea, itching, fevers, tiredness, and loss of appetite. Of course, such symptoms may also be due to definite physical illness, but more often they are not. Stomach aches, for example, are nine times out of ten due to tension. There are also many illnesses brought about in the first place by physical disease, but where tension or other forms of upset or distress can make things worse, for example, diabetes, asthma, or eczema. Some illnesses in children can be brought on purely by psychological factors, for example, migraine, ulcers, and high blood pressure.

All in the mind?

In thinking about psychosomatic reactions, it is important to make a few points clear:

1. No psychosomatic problem is imagined or deliberately brought

A tension stomach ache is an example of a psychosomatic reaction. Worry and anxiety (emotions) about starting school, for example, can produce spasms in your child's abdomen.

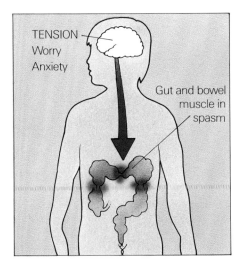

TENSION
Worry
Anxiety

Gut and bowel muscle in spasm

on. They are all absolutely genuine and not 'just in the mind'.

2. Because a child has a psychosomatic disorder, it does not mean that he is emotionally disturbed or psychologically maladjusted. Remember, it is normal for people to experience psychologically-induced physical symptoms. There can be few of us who have not experienced 'tension headaches', palpitations, 'butterflies' in the stomach when nervous, or perhaps an increased need to go to the toilet. It is well-recognized that those children with psychosomatic ailments often seem to be the most stable, well-behaved and conscientious, which leads us on the the third point.

Why and how do they occur?

Why do such seemingly well-adjusted children react in this way? Indeed, why does anyone react in this way? The answer is unfortunately complicated. Life is made up of a wide and continuing variety of experiences some of which are exciting, happy or pleasurable, while others are boring, irritating, upsetting, unhappy or worrying. Throughout life, then, you and your child are continuously having your emotions aroused (emotional arousal), sometimes pleasantly and sometimes unpleasantly. The part of the brain concerned with emotion, the hypothalamus, is right next to a small gland, the pituitary, which despite its size, plays a vital part in the control of a wide range of your body's functions. There are many nerve pathways between the hypothalamus and

The pituitary gland in the brain plays a vital role in controlling many body functions including physical reactions to emotion, such as headaches and stomach aches.

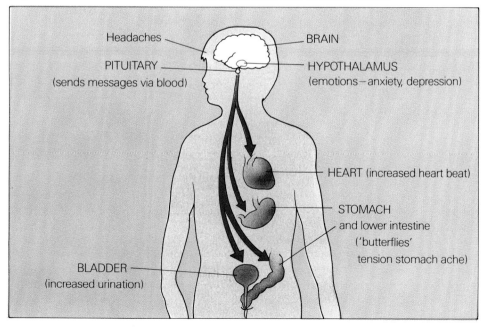

Headaches

BRAIN

PITUITARY
(sends messages via blood)

HYPOTHALAMUS
(emotions—anxiety, depression)

HEART (increased heart beat)

STOMACH
and lower intestine
('butterflies'
tension stomach ache)

BLADDER
(increased urination)

pituitary (see diagram on page 79). So you can see, even without any great knowledge of human anatomy and physiology, how easy it is for emotional arousal to produce physical symptoms or even physical disorders.

Vulnerability

Because emotional arousal can so easily lead to physical symptoms, you can understand why your child may develop a psychosomatic disorder. He may have been born with a tendency to develop the condition. For example, eczema is due to being born with a skin which is sensitive (allergic) to various substances. At times when your emotions are aroused, your skin becomes even more sensitive. I shall deal with this more fully on page 83.

Bottled-up feelings

Many children, though they may not have a weakness towards a particular disorder, nonetheless develop psychosomatic symptoms like headaches, stomach aches or vomiting. Doctors know from the evidence that many such children are somehow less able to show their feelings in the same way as other children, for example, they rarely cry, or become angry, or express sadness, and instead they develop physical symptoms. Of course, it is not quite as straightforward as this, because many children show their emotions openly and have physical symptoms. Nonetheless, it is surprising how often children with psychosomatic problems tend to bottle-up their feelings (as do their parents) and are described as self-contained, quiet, stable, well-behaved, and so on. As a matter of interest, some research has shown that delinquent children tend not to suffer from psychosomatic disorders. It may well be that when delinquents

express their feeling openly in their bad behaviour, they protect themselves from much physical illness!

To illustrate some of these points, it may be helpful to give some examples:

Ten-year-old Andrea was having many severe headaches. Investigations showed there was no physical cause. When I met her with her family I noticed that although everyone was kind and considerate there was obvious tension and anger in the family, none of which was openly expressed. Andrea's father told me that he suffered severe migraines but he never told the family about the worries that brought these on because he did not want to upset them. I encouraged the family to express themselves much more openly, in particular to talk to each other about their worries and the things that annoyed them such as father's pipe-smoking, and mother always tidying up (trivial habits like these are the main causes of irritation and stress in families). As they learned to do this, so both Andrea's and her father's headaches lessened, until eventually both were free of them. No harm comes from people having an occasional moan!

Eight-year-old Penny's severe asthma was not responding to treatment as well as would be expected. During my talks with Penny's mother she told me that her husband had died of asthma when Penny was a baby. She had never been able to discuss him with Penny because she was frightened this would make her asthma worse. With no real information about her father, Penny had built up a distorted and frightening picture of what had happened, and was convinced she would also die soon. Once they talked openly about father, her asthma rapidly improved.

Peter, six years old, was caught up in his parents' continuous arguments, with each parent trying to get him to side with them against the other. This continuing division of loyalty and affection produced so much stress that it caused Peter to have periodic bouts of vomiting – for which no physical cause could be found. The vomiting only stopped when his parents were able to recognize what was happening and stopped asking Peter to take sides.

Jim, aged eleven, developed stomach aches soon after transferring schools. His mother had been depressed for several months. When Jim was seen by a paediatrician, no physical cause was found for his pain. However, when his teachers were approached, they commented that he had seemed very worried. After talks, we discovered that Jim had become very anxious about his mother's health, and it seems the pains had served the purpose of keeping him at home where he could keep an eye on his mother. Such episodes are quite common in children who have sick parents and can also happen when they have just transferred schools.

Sarah, aged fifteen, developed aches and pains all over her body so intense that for a while her mother thought she must have a serious illness. Tests showed nothing wrong. A sympathetic nurse spent quite a while chatting with her. She discovered that Sarah was very upset because her boyfriend had said that if she did not go to bed with him, he would stop seeing her. Sarah was frightened of getting pregnant, and of what her parents would say if they found out she was having sex. The nurse advised Sarah to talk to her mother about it. Sarah's mother felt upset that she had not realized that Sarah had been worried, but with some prompting from the hospital staff, she and Sarah discussed the problems. Eventually, after much talking, Sarah decided to give up her boyfriend. Her pains disappeared.

Clearly, Sarah was not ready for the responsibility of a sexual relationship, and had not felt able to turn to her parents for help.

These children all had rather more severe psychosomatic symptoms, which had to be dealt with at the hospital. Most children at some time have signs of a psychosomatic illness that does not necessarily mean there is any deeper underlying problem. The illness is simply a way of expressing feelings, and especially the less pleasant ones such as tensions, worries, boredom and sadness. Do remember that this is a normal process and nothing to be ashamed of, or unduly worried by.

What to do if your child has a psychosomatic problem

The answer depends on a number of points such as how severe the problem is, and how often it arises.

First I will describe what you should do when your child only occasionally has psychosomatic symptoms such as headaches, stomach aches, limb pains, vomiting, or dizzy spells. So long as your doctor has said that they are no signs of an underlying physical disorder, you should then see whether there is a pattern to the symptoms. The next stage is to try to take steps to remedy the situation. Suppose, for example, your child is having particular difficulties with one lesson or a teacher at school. You should discuss his problem with that teacher, and decide what can be done. On the other hand, if whatever is causing the trouble (illness of a parent, for example) just cannot be avoided, then your child needs help to express his understandable reactions in words, or if very young, in play. Always adopt a sympathetic and understanding attitude which will enable your child to feel safe enough to 'talk out' his problems. The emphasis should be away from the symptoms and towards the difficulties. Remember, also, the problems probably won't disappear with one talk. It's a gradual process.

When it's more serious

When the pain, rash or other physical symptom is more persistant it usually means that the underlying problem is a more serious one. Your child may be generally unhappy; he may not be coping with school work, or he may be having difficulty making or keeping friends. He may be worried about you or some family problem. He may not be receiving as much attention, affection or stimulation as he needs, or the opposite – he may be getting too much!

Seeking advice – and taking it

It is understandable that many parents whose children have physical symptoms that don't clear up seek further medical help. Often they ask for a specialist's opinion, and then a third opinion, finding it hard to believe that there is no physical cause. Contrary to what they intend, such parents are not acting in their child's best interests, as they are seeking a solution that does not exist. Nor, on the other hand, will ignoring the symptoms solve the problem. It is important, under these circumstances, to accept professional help in unravelling the problem and finding the best way of helping your child. Your doctor may wish to help directly or recommend a child guidance clinic, paediatrician or psychiatrist, for a more detailed assessment. There is no need to be ashamed of the need for psychiatric help. It doesn't mean that you or your child is neurotic, disturbed or mad, but simply that there is a complicated problem that requires this kind of specialized help to unravel and resolve it (see Chapter ten, 'talking treatment').

When emotional factors make definite illnesses worse

Many children suffer from particular illnesses in which emotions play an important part. Among these are asthma, eczema, diabetes, peptic ulcer, bowel inflammation, epilepsy, migraine and arthritis. Each of these are first and foremost illnesses, but strong emotions may well make the illness worse. When this happens, remember, it is a natural process and doesn't in any way imply that you are a bad parent. For your child to feel strong emotions is normal, and no attempt should be made to protect your child from them. It is an important part of growing up to allow your child to experience a large range of emotions and learn how to deal with them. If you have an ill child who is excited, bored, sad, or angry, you should handle him as if he were healthy, and remain calm, caring and reassuring. Emotional attempts to damp-down someone else's feelings will not succeed. Far better for your child to get it off his chest.

Your own feelings

The same goes for you as the parent of a sick child. You should not feel you have to keep all your feelings under control. All parents at times feel tired, fed-up, or worried, and then it is not possible to be as loving, attentive and confident as you might wish. You may try and conceal your more immediate feelings, and you may or may not be successful. However, if you bottle up such feelings you will feel tense, and your child will sense this. He will be puzzled and distressed by the confusing picture of a parent who claims to feel fine and who clearly does not. Not only that, he will learn that feelings should be bottled-up, which is rarely helpful. At the same time, it is important for a parent who does feel very worried about a sick child to share those anxieties with another adult, friend, relative or professional person who can help get things into proportion. Most parents will want to be well-informed about their child's illness so that they can give the child as much help as they are capable of. As well as a talk with your doctor, there are many excellent books that will give much practical help and advice, such as *Asthma and Hayfever* by Dr Allan Knight, and other books in this series.

Before ending this chapter I want to mention three problems which are both complicated and confusing, and which have a psychosomatic component: allergies, obesity, and anorexia nervosa.

Allergy

Many children have allergies – the exact numbers are not known. Children (and, indeed, adults) can be allergic to very many different substances including foods, dust, animals and medicines. Allergies can cause reactions in any part of the body such as the skin, the lungs, the gut, the nervous system, or the blood vessels. Often allergy runs in families. The most topical allergy is food allergy.

Make sure it is an allergy

Most allergies are diagnosed by skin tests. If there is any doubt, doctors can carry out what is called a 'challenge' – the suspected allergen is introduced, preferably in disguised form, and any reactions to it are carefully watched for. The disguise is important because the power of suggestion can create an identical reaction to that thought to be caused by the allergy. Indeed, this is where the psychosomatic angle needs careful consideration. Reactions to tension or emotional upset can be exactly the same as allergic reactions.

Psychosomatic reactions are very much more common than allergic reactions. Tragically, some parents are so convinced that their child's symptoms are allergic that they go to extreme lengths to convince others, and are often unable to see what is obvious to an outsider. Such children may be put on strange, and sometimes unhealthy diets, or prevented from leading normal lives because of their parents' misguided fears. Such actions invariably make the situation worse. Suspected allergy is one of those illnesses where it is better not to do-it-yourself.

Even if an illness is caused in the first place by an allergy, it is not at all uncommon for psychological factors to play a part. This is particularly true when going to great lengths to avoid contact with the allergen becomes an important part of the child's life.

What do you do if your child is allergic?

Your doctor will advise you about this. Usually keeping clear of whatever is causing the allergy is suffi-

Allergens

Animal fur e.g. horses', cats', dogs'
Pollens
Metals e.g. nickel, chrome
Plastics
Cosmetics
Certain foods e.g. wheat, cow's milk, eggs, fish, nuts, caffeine
Certain medicines e.g. penicillin, aspirin.

Possible allergens that are known to cause allergic reactions in a certain percentage of children.

cient. Sometimes this is not always possible, such as a dust-allergy or certain food allergies. In these cases, your doctor may prescribe certain medicines for your child – these are usually helpful and harmless. Do try and help your child to lead as normal a life as possible. Remember, though, that he may be worried about his allergy, or anything else for that matter, and will need to talk about it. If worries are not recognized, then they can get bottled-up and may come out as symptoms just like the allergy!

What if the doctor says no allergy exists?
Accept his advice, even though you may find it hard to believe. Continuing to seek an allergen, or treating a child as if he is allergic, will almost certainly make his condition worse. If your child has mysterious symptoms which are not due to allergy or other physical causes, then it is extremely likely that he has a psychosomatic reaction. This needs the correct treatment just as much as any purely physical disorder. That is why you should seek the help of a psychiatrist. Understanding the stresses that are affecting your child, and either helping him to cope, or if possible lessening them, are just as important as any medicine.

Obesity
About 10 per cent of children in developed countries are so overweight that they are described as obese, that is, they have excessive body fat. Obesity, which affects boys and girls equally, is nearly always due to:

Overeating Quite simply, such children eat far too much and become obese. There is nothing physically wrong with them, but the overeating usually starts early in life and often stems from emotional problems (see Chapter two). The tendency of these children is to eat when in distress, as a way of comforting themselves. They are often tall for their age, but are most easily recognized by their enormous appetites.

Some obese children (and adults) suffer from:

Poor metabolism of fat This means that although your child does not necessarily eat too much, his body does not easily get rid of fat. The fat stays in the body and the child becomes obese. Such children often have obese relatives, as the problem tends to run in families. In my experience, overeating very commonly occurs in this group as well.

Glandular (or endocrine) disorder Very rarely indeed is obesity due to something serious such as an abnormality in the endocrine glands. These children nearly always have other problems such as being short, or slow in their development. These conditions are easily recognized by doctors.

What should you do if your child is obese?
Because obesity can have a bad effect on future health, often leading to heart and lung problems, it is important to seek help. Because it is so rare, your doctor will almost certainly be able to assure you that your child has no glandular problem. In that case, he will recommend a diet, and perhaps a programme of exercise. It is important that you should make sure that the diet is stuck to.

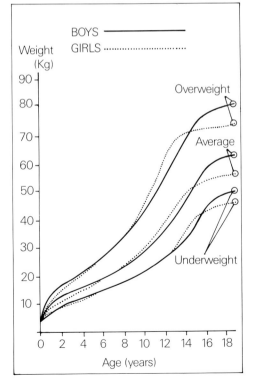

A combined weight chart for boys and girls. The normal weight range lies between the top and bottom curve, the middle curve representing the ideal average weight for each sex. Above the top curve, your child is overweight and below the bottom curve, your child is underweight.

Like adults, children often hate diets. The only way to be certain that the diet is stuck to is by regular weighing. At first, you can record the weight daily, and after a couple of weeks weigh him less frequently.

Your child will enjoy having a large and colourful chart which will show his weight going down. Small rewards (not sweets) for small amounts of weight-loss will also encourage dieting. Work out a schedule that will earn him rewards two or three times a week. Providing the diet allows for more calories being used up than taken in, he must lose weight. A 1,000 calorie diet is about right for most children. You should discuss the diet with your doctor or dietitian.

What if dieting does not work?
Sadly, most obese children do not respond well to dieting. The main reason for this is that they do not stick to the diet. I see many children who swear they are sticking to their diet but are still gaining weight. When they come into the hospital where we can be certain that the diet is stuck to, they almost always lose weight.

The best thing to do if your child is more than 25 lb (11 kg) overweight and not losing weight on a diet is to ask for him to spend a short time in hospital. This should at least improve the situation for the moment. Ideally, your child will then learn healthier eating habits, which he can maintain when he returns home. Unfortunately, very many children go back to their old habits when they leave the hospital. There is a tremendous burden on parents at that stage to become much firmer with their child.

Check for an emotional cause
Besides using diet, exercise and rewards, you should look into the possibility that your child's overeating is a response to distress, boredom or worry. If you think it might be, then a child psychologist or psychiatrist may be able to help, and you should seek their advice. This is especially important for your child as obesity can itself be distressing, leading to teasing and isolation. This can be so upsetting that he may console himself by eating more.

Above all, try not to convince yourself that there must be an undiscovered physical cause. Obesity is due to eating more than the body needs. It is unfortunate that some people get fatter far more easily than others. If they are to avoid later health problems, though, they must find ways of eating less.

Anorexia nervosa
This is a puzzling condition that affects predominantly girls and women between the ages of fourteen and twenty-five. It does, rarely, occur in younger girls, and sometimes in boys. The cause is not known, but there is no evidence that it is due to any physical disorder. Usually, there seems to be a number of factors working together such as family stresses. Social pressures can also play a part, especially where advertising models show the ideal female proportions of protruding cheeks and hip bones. The problem often starts after a chance remark about weight. Sometimes, it only becomes a problem after a period of 'normal slimming'.

Anorexia sufferers become obsessionally preoccupied with their weight and how much they eat. They desperately try to remain very thin, even when they are emaciated. Many have the idea that they are overweight even when everyone else can see that they are obviously underweight. They may have a poor appetite, though some have normal appetites which they try to overcome. If they fail, they then have eating binges (this is sometimes called bulimia) after which they try to make themselves vomit. In desperate attempts to lose weight, some anorectics use laxatives, or take excessive exercise. Interest in food and even enthusiastic cooking for others is common.

What should be done?
This is a very serious, complicated and life-threatening condition. Urgent treatment is essential, usually in hospital. If you think your child may have anorexia nervosa, seek help immediately. Don't allow yourself to be put off getting help. The longer you leave it, the more serious it becomes, and the harder it is to treat. Caught early, gradual re-feeding and family therapy is the most effective treatment (see Chapter ten). If not treated early then the outlook is poor, and hospitalization is essential.

Getting psychosomatic illness into perspective

Mild psychosomatic symptoms are commonplace. Such symptoms are nothing to be ashamed of and are not due to your being a bad parent or to any serious psychological disturbance. You should try hard to find out what is worrying or upsetting your child. If you refuse to accept a psychosomatic explanation, when this is what your doctor has diagnosed, you may prolong the problem. Whatever the symptoms or illness, try to help your child to lead as normal a life as possible, following medical advice on such matters as diet, medicine and activities. With the right sort of handling, most symptoms disappear in due course, while the specific illnesses such as asthma will run a far calmer course. Psychiatric help can be very valuable and should be sought if your child is having more problems, emotional or physical, than is usual in your child's kind of illness.

8. CHANGES IN A CHILD'S WORLD

Every child is exposed from time to time to a change in routine or circumstance. These changes may be relatively small and insignificant, large and important, temporary or permanent. What is to you quite a small change can seem to your young child like something enormous and long-lasting. For example, you might be confined to bed with influenza for a couple of days, but this can be very distressing for your child. Suddenly, a parent who normally seems all-powerful is apparently helpless. It can seem as if the world is coming to an end. Another example could be when your child goes to playgroup or nursery school at the age of three. It may be the first time he has spent a morning away from you. It can be a frightening and lonely experience. The birth of a brother or sister to a toddler may at first be a time of excitement. Soon, however, he may notice that his parents are more tired than usual, distracted, perhaps irritable and probably spending a lot of their time with the new baby. Such events can happen in most households, and are likely to have an effect on most young children.

Less predictable changes

Among other less predictable events that may occur are:

- Your child may need to go into the hospital
- Your family may move
- Your marriage may be under stress or even break up
- Tensions can build up due to unemployment or financial difficulties
- Serious ill health or the death of close relatives may occur
- The death of a pet can be upsetting
- Re-marriage and the arrival of a step-parent, or step-brother or -sister can create much tension
- The loss of a parent can be particularly devastating.

The list is endless.

How might your child react to change?

This depends on many factors: your child's age, his temperament, the type of change, whether or not it is expected, and whether and how you prepare him for it; they can all play a part.

Regression – a sort of going backwards in development is one of the most common reactions. Skills that have been acquired are temporarily lost: a child who is dry at night, might start wetting his bed, for example. It may be that a toddler who has learned to use a cup, suddenly reverts to a bottle.

Clinging is another reaction. Your child may become much more demanding, cling to you, and fuss if you try to get on with your own tasks.

Rejection is the opposite of clinging. If your child has to suffer a major stress such as being separated from you for a few days, he may respond to your return by ignoring you. This is not uncommon in young children who go into the hospital without a parent. At first, he may protest, making an enormous fuss; after a while, realizing that you are not immediately returning, he may become withdrawn and miserable, almost in a state of despair. When he finally sees you, he may ignore you, as if you are not there. The younger he is, the harder it is for him to understand why you should (apparently) abandon him.

Changing affections Another way of reacting is for a child to change his affections, becoming more attached to one parent than another. Changes can cause older children to become defiant and disobedient or sullen and withdrawn. Many children react to stressful changes by developing aches and pains or other physical symptoms. Commonly, these can include stomach aches, headaches, loss of appetite, change in bowel habit, nausea and vomiting. Almost any physical symptom can occur in response to stress. This kind of reaction is discussed in more detail in Chapter seven.

Delayed reaction Sometimes, children do not show any obvious reaction to a change in their routine, or relationships, but more often than not the distress shows through eventually:

Alison, aged twelve, had been very close to her grandmother who died suddenly from a stroke. Apart from being obviously upset on the day she was told, she seemed to recover quickly from the shock. Some weeks later, however, Alison's teacher informed her parents that her schoolwork had deteriorated considerably and that she had seemed very distracted.

Sometimes a child's behaviour changes for no obvious reason and he becomes a worry to his parents. But when that happens there is always a cause, or more often a combination of causes:

Alan, aged fourteen, had been born slightly clumsy and had had difficulty with spelling. Nonetheless, he had been a cheerful and popular boy until the age of thirteen. Gradually, he became bad-tempered and argumentative. He started overeating. He resented going to school. Eventually, his parents sought help. It transpired that his father had been under great presssure at work, and had been returning home tired and irritable. Around the same time, Alan had changed schools, and his new classmates teased him about his clumsiness and called him 'spastic'.

In Alan's case, two changes had occurred at the sensitive time of entering adolescence, when he was particularly vulnerable. It is possible that any one of these stresses alone may have had no effect, but the combination was too much.

How to handle stress reactions to change
While in Chapter nine I discuss in general terms how to help your child cope with various stresses, here I outline particular steps you can take.

These steps are indicated in the diagram overleaf.

Anticipation

Many changes and their stress reactions are forseeable and can therefore be prepared for. I have already outlined the events that are liable to be most stressful for children. Your awareness of these can allow you to prepare your child for those that can be anticipated.

Preparation

When changes do occur your child is likely to cope far better if he is well prepared. How you prepare him depends on his age and what you are preparing him for:

Graham, aged five, had to go into the hospital to have his tonsils removed. A week before the operation his mother took him to the hospital, and the nursing staff showed him around the ward and explained what would happen. His parents bought a booklet that told in story-form about the procedures Graham would experience, and read it with him. The hospitalization and operation proved successful

In contrast, the parents of Richard, also five, thought he would worry too much if they told him that he would be having an operation. When the time came to go into hospital, he was told he was going for an X-ray, and then found himself in a hospital bed. He was terrified and cried for several hours. After he finally left the hospital he became very clinging, refused to go to school, and wet his bed. It took six months for him to return to normal.

It does not pay to conceal the truth

from children when it concerns them; in general, honesty is the best policy.

Recognizing and understanding reactions

Whether or not an important change in your child's life has been expected, if you can recognize and understand his reactions to it, you can then help him to cope.

Greg, aged nine, had never been a worry to his parents. Seemingly out of the blue, he became irritable, could not settle to sleep at night, and would constantly argue with other family members. Initially, no one could work out what was wrong, and his family became irritated in return. This only aggravated the situation. After one particularly stormy episode, his mother had a long talk with him and helped him tell her what was wrong. His class teacher was on prolonged sick-leave and the replacement had a very different style of teaching and discipline. She had made a number of adverse comments about Greg's work and he felt he was being singled out. In retrospect, his parents recalled that he was always slightly irritable at the beginning of each school year.

Acknowledging and reassuring

Whatever the change and whatever the reaction, one of the most helpful things you can do for your child is to let him know you understand how he feels about it. Simple statements such as 'Oh you poor dear, how terrible for you' may sound facile or trite out of context, but for your child they convey far more than just words. A sympathetic acknowledgement helps your child feel misunderstood and accepted.

90

If, on the other hand, he gets the message from you that he is wrong, or that he should not feel that way, then he is liable to feel misunderstood, isolated and somehow in the wrong. Inevitably it is then harder for him to cope with the change and his own reaction.

Seeking solutions

Many children cope quite well with the stresses caused by change well once their reactions have been recognized, understood and acknowledged, and they have been reassured:

During the chat Greg had with his mother he had a good cry, and she sympathized with how he felt. She explained that different teachers do have different ways of teaching, and that she thought he was okay and that his work and behaviour were fine. Following this, Greg seemed to revert to normal quite quickly.

Sometimes, something more is required. If Greg had not settled, his parents may have needed to go to the school to discuss the problem with his teacher. In some instances, definite steps can be taken.

Diane, aged three, enjoyed the arrival of her baby brother at first. She had been involved in much of the preparation including helping her mother choose some clothes and toys. Her father read her a story about a girl of three whose mother had a baby, which described the sorts of things that happened. Diane visited her mother and brother in hospital and was even allowed to hold him (with help). A couple of weeks later she started having temper-tantrums, would not eat and threw her food from the table. Clearly, she was reacting to the major changes in her home. Her parents did their best to comfort and reassure her, but this did not seem enough. She did improve, however, when her mother encouraged her to help wash and feed him and change his diapers.

In this way, Diane had been helped to feel important again at a time when she was feeling rejected. Her parents had found the obvious solution. It is not always quite so easy to find the right answer, but following the steps outlined will certainly put you on the right path. If you are not successful, do not hesitate to seek help (see Chapter ten).

How to handle the loss or impending loss of a close relative

It is difficult to imagine how upsetting the loss of a loved one can be for a child. My advice, nevertheless, is to give your child the facts as clearly as you can, whether the lost one is a parent, brother, sister, grandparent or any other close relative.

It is not possible to generalize about the psychological effects of loss. Inevitably, children of various ages show their distress in different ways.

Very young children may be unable to appreciate that the loss of a parent or close relative is permanent, and often ask 'When is daddy coming back?' They may compensate for the loss by imagining they have seen the lost parent, or that they are going to see him or her very soon. Older children may at first react with disbelief, but soon become very saddened and shocked. Later, they may become withdrawn and depressed, even despairing. Many children quite illogically blame themselves for the death of a loved one. Sometimes

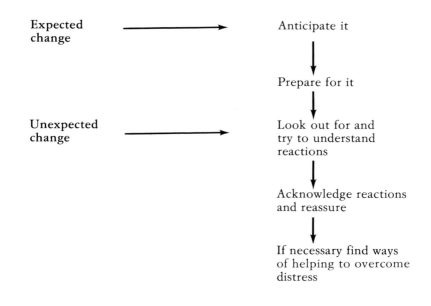

Expected change → Anticipate it → Prepare for it

Unexpected change → Look out for and try to understand reactions → Acknowledge reactions and reassure → If necessary find ways of helping to overcome distress

Some guidelines to help you handle your child's stress reactions to change.

children express anger either at the surviving relatives or the lost relative themselves. Gradually, over a period of six to twelve months, most children recover, although it may be years before readjustment is complete.

Expressing grief

It is best to allow and even encourage your child to express his distress. In this way, he is most likely eventually to resolve his grief. A child who bottles it all up has the grief inside him, and is liable to remain distressed. I advise parents to encourage their children to talk about the 'lost' parent. It helps to be totally honest about what has happened. Many children value looking at and keeping photographs and talking about the dead parent. If there is a grave to visit, then this is often well worthwhile. Some parents think this is macabre, but it helps children if they know where the dead parent is buried. Whether or not you believe in

heaven, many children do, and if yours does it is helpful in the process of grieving to be able to think of the parent being in a safe and pleasant place.

Jenny, aged seven, appeared at first not to be particularly distressed by her mother's death. After a few weeks, however, it became clear that she had lost weight. She was also clinging to her father, could not concentrate at school and was no longer interested in television or her friends. She was often angry when adults tried to comfort her, and she told her father she thought it was her fault that Mummy had died. Her father and her teacher were both able to accept all her behaviour as a natural reaction to her mother's death. They acknowledged her distress by simply stating that they knew how sad she felt, and they did not argue with her when she had angry outbursts. After four months, she had clearly started getting better.

A dying relative

When it is known that a parent or other close relative is dying, there is no absolute best way of helping a child to cope. I feel that whenever possible it is better to be open and honest. It is bad enough that death is impending, but if it cannot be discussed then the child is likely to feel more isolated, frightened and confused. I find it useful to talk openly about what is happening, and what is likely to happen in the future, whatever the age of the child.

Divorce

The loss of a parent need not be through death, but when one parent leaves home through divorce. In this situation honesty is invariably the best policy. Children do value an explanation such as 'Mummy and Daddy aren't happy living together any more, so we've decided that it's better if one of us goes to live somewhere else'.

Contact with the children Parents should make every effort to let their children have as much contact as possible with both of them. However bitter the separation, they should, for their children's sake, avoid attacking each other in front of the children, or using the children as part of a continuing battle.

Mr and Mrs S. separated after years of disharmony. They could not agree on how often and where and when Mr S. should see his sons Peter, aged nine, and Philip, aged seven. They argued bitterly over every point. Eventually, both boys became very distressed. When they were with their mother, they said they hated their father, but when with their father they told him they hated their mother (a common reaction to continuing fighting after separation). Philip started soiling his pants and refusing to go to school, while Peter developed frequent stomach aches.

Understand your child's feelings The parent who has left home should try to make sure that they see their children on a regular basis. It is awful for children if they do not know when next they will see their father (or mother). Both parents will have to face the fact that their children will frequently feel angry with them for separating. They may blame one parent more than the other, and may try to make one parent feel that he or she is not as kind and generous as the other. Alternatively, as with Peter and Philip, they may side with whichever parent they happen to be with at the time.

If you recognize the existence of all these possibilities, you will be better prepared to handle them if they do occur. Remember that your child needs to express his despair, anger, and resentment, and that by trying to talk him out of it, he is liable to feel that no one understands, and then he'll be more unhappy. Far better to acknowledge and accept the feelings, show your understanding, and then get on with things as best you can.

Should you separate? Parents often stay together 'for the sake of the children'. This is a noble idea, but is only justified if the marital problems are not too severe. If you are unhappy together, often arguing, or worse, the children are likely to be better off in the long run if you do separate.

What about step-familes?

If a divorced parent re-marries, then children have to adjust not only to having a new adult around, but often step-brothers and step-sisters also. Later, further children may be born, so that there are then half-brothers or sisters to contend with. No child can calmly accept such a dramatic change. It is pointless to expect that your child will happily accept a 'new parent', let alone actually 'love' that person. Far more likely, he will resent the intrusion, fight to reject the intruder, and certainly do his best to get between his parent and the 'rival'. The same applies to step- and half-brothers and sisters.

Providing, again, that you are aware of these possibilities you will be in a stronger position to cope. Try to handle him in the same way as you would any of his other stress reactions to change or loss.

Four points for coping with change

- When changes are expected, try to prepare your child.
- When a change has happened, look out for and try to understand your child's reactions.
- Acknowledge, comfort and reassure; then find ways of overcoming his distress.
- If in doubt, seek professional help.

9. GOOD-ENOUGH PARENTING

All parents want to be good parents, and give their children the very best. This can be a very difficult task, for children grow and change so quickly and each new stage can bring another set of problems. I am often asked what should be done in particular circumstances, what is normal, what is to be expected? Sometimes it is possible to give a very definite answer; on other occasions I can only make general comments. Fortunately, most parents do the right thing instinctively. They are 'good enough' parents. A famous British paediatrician and psychoanalyst, Donald Winnicott, coined the phrase 'good-enough mothering'. He used the term to refer to a mother's ability to recognize and respond to her child's needs, without necessarily having to be a perfect mother who does everything right, all the time. Now that men have been liberated, it seems reasonable to talk about 'good-enough parenting'; in other words, the ability of both parents to recognize and respond to a child's needs.

Assuming parenting is 'good enough', most behavioural or emotional problems that arise can be short-lived. Inevitably, there will be some problems that are a result of ill-health, personality idiosyncracies, extreme shyness, or major traumas such as a loss of a loved one. Even so, good-enough parenting can help many such children to cope relatively satisfactorily, and is the key to helping a child with emotional and behavioural problems.

What is good-enough parenting?

Being able to recognize and respond to a child's needs involves knowing what those needs may be, when they are likely to arise, and how to respond to them. Needs change as time goes by, and good-enough parents have a rough idea of what is appropriate and what is not, at any particular age. Here, in broad outlines, are the tasks involved in good-enough parenting:

- Providing basic physical needs
- Providing emotional bonds and relationships
- Providing a secure base
- Guiding and controlling behaviour
- Providing normal life experiences
- Teaching communication
- Helping your child to be part of a family.

Providing basic physical needs
This involves attending to the most basic of a child's needs, feeding, clothing, warmth, hygiene. Without fulfilment of these needs, a child's emotional and physical health is obviously at risk (see Chapter two).

Providing emotional bonds and relationships

Babies and children need a close, warm and loving relationship with at least one person, from the first few weeks of life. There has been considerable argument among experts about whether this person must be the child's mother or father. In fact, the biological link is not essential, and the adult can equally be an adoptive or foster-parent. What matters most is that the person is on the scene very early in the child's life, occupies the central part of the child's life and is permanent. Of course, two adults can fulfil the criteria, though inevitably very early in life it is more likely to be the mother.

This close relationship or 'bonding' is a necessary part of any child's healthy physical and emotional development. The essence of any close relationship and certainly of that between parent and child is to help the child feel good about himself.

Providing a secure base

This means a stable home and a stable family life. Providing a stable and secure base allows the child to develop sound healthy emotions. When family relationships are unhappy and disrupted, for example through several marital problems, then a wide range of emotional and behavioural difficulties are likely to arise.

Guiding and controlling behaviour

There is no right way to bring up children, and indeed there are considerable differences in the way children are reared throughout the world. There are, however, some useful guidelines:

Consistency and flexibility In general, you need to be consistent in your approach to your child, though

Babies and children need a close, warm and loving relationship with at least one parent from the first few weeks of life.

allowing flexibility. Too much flexibility can create uncertainty for your child who then becomes confused about what is right and what is wrong. Too rigid an approach prevents natural exploration and individuality. Ultimately, it can lead to a teenage backlash with a rejection of your values.

The flexible parent is neither overprotective nor underprotective, neither too harsh nor too soft, neither too rigid nor too pliable. You adjust your responses according to the demands of the situation, and the age and needs of your child. For example, you would allow your two-year-old child to explore a new room and play with toys he finds, but you would stop him from examining an electric socket or a pot of hot coffee. You would, when crossing a busy road, carry your child if he is two years old, hold his hand firmly if he is under six or seven, and still insist on his remaining close to you even up to the age of ten or eleven.

Inconsistency Inevitably, all parents are inconsistent at times. For example, what you can tolerate in the way of noise one day, you may find intolerable the next. You are not failing as a parent when you are sometimes inconsistent. Children get to recognize their parents' inconsistencies and idiosyncracies. Providing the basic relationship is satisfactory, they seem to adjust to them. Problems only really arise when you are too flexible or rigid or when there is frequent and intense inconsistency – for example, if on one day you allow your three-year-old child to throw food around, the next day you smack him for doing it, and the third day you ignore it again, he can never know what is expected.

Rewards and punishments You shape your child's behaviour by how much you reward or punish him. Rewards include simply paying attention, praising, cuddling, or the giving of something he likes. Punishment can involve ignoring, scolding, smacking (or worse), being sent out of the room, or the withdrawal of something important.

You are constantly rewarding or punishing your child, whether knowingly or unknowingly, by the kind of immediate response you make to any aspect of his behaviour. So, if you laugh or cuddle him when he does something you approve of, you are in fact encouraging him to do it again. If, however, you ignore him when he does something you approve of, he may get the message you are not interested and so not do it again.

Reward rather than punish In general, it is much better to reward than punish. Plenty of attention is a far more effective way of encouraging the right or desirable behaviour than ignoring, or punishing in other ways, the wrong or undesirable behaviour. (Ignoring involves paying no attention, punishment involves taking definite action against your child, such as telling him off.) Occasionally undesirable behaviour cannot be ignored, for example, if your slightly jealous two-year-old is rough with a younger brother or sister.

Providing normal life experiences To help your child mature and eventually cope as an independent adult, you have to provide him with certain experiences. Children need to be loved, cuddled, played with and talked to. As they grow they need to know how to mix with others, how to get along on their own, and how to learn. The child who is not talked to cannot learn to understand or speak.

The child who is not cuddled and loved cannot form relationships with others. The child who is not helped to separate from his parents will not be able to lead an independent life.

Most parents instinctively provide these experiences in a natural way.

Coping with a change (see also Chapter eight) Problems occasionally arise at times of transition. For example, it can be hard for a parent who is used to a very close relationship with a five-year-old to encourage him to cope with going off to school, especially if the child is understandably anxious. A different sort of separation occurs in adolescence. Here the child usually wants more independence than many parents can tolerate. The good-enough parent understands these needs, and provides the right amount of control, not too much, nor too little.

Unpleasant and unexpected things can happen, for example, illness or accidents. As parents you cannot change these but you can help your child to cope. You will need to be flexible, and understanding. Equally important, you have to help your child to understand his own reactions and cope with them.

Teaching communication
Everyone needs to be able to speak and to understand. But communication involves more than these basics. It includes being able to put thoughts into words and to give names to feelings. It involves expressing complicated ideas, and talking about things that are sometimes hard to talk about, like fears or angers. It involves recognizing the meaning of facial expressions when words are not being used. The good-enough parent teaches her child to do all this. You start the process early simply by talking to your child, long

before he develops understanding. As he grows, you put names to objects and respond to his behaviour with more words. When he is in distress you give him names for the emotion he is experiencing – sad, frightened, angry. As well as naming it, you accept it, and acknowledge it; you do not pass judgment on it, or deny it, or tell him he should not feel that way.

In other words, you recognize that your child experiences the full range of human emotions, that they are a natural and necessary part of being alive, and you help him to cope with them and understand them as natural and necessary.

The following sequences may serve as an example.

Jeremy, aged three, is refusing to stay in his room at bedtime. His mother is beginning to feel exasperated but suspects she knows the reason why he is unable to settle.

Mother – Jeremy, I want you to stay in your room.
Jeremy – No, shan't.
Mother – Do you want to tell me why?
Jeremy – No, don't know.
Mother – Do you think it's unfair that I'm with Chris (baby brother aged six months)?
Jeremy – No, I don't care.
Mother – Well I think I'd care if I was you (cuddles him).
Jeremy – Why can't I come down?
Mother – Look, I know you'd like to be with me, like Chris, and I know you feel a bit angry. I would too. But I do love you, and if you stay in your room, when I've finished feeding Chris I'll come and cuddle you.
Jeremy – Do you love me, Mummy?
Mother – Of course I love you very much. I have to look after

Chris as well, because he's very little, but you're my favourite big boy.

Jeremy's mother has recognized his distress, and has not tried to get rid of it. On the contrary, she has accepted it as justified, and shown she understands. Having done this, she gently explains and then reassures.

Talking through worries

As your child gets older, you help him to talk about problems he has, things that are worrying or upsetting him. You are aware of potential areas of stress and watch out for them, and how they may show. You know that, just as adults can and do frequently get tension headaches, so your child can get tension stomach aches or indeed aches and pains anywhere in his body. You learn to recognize these for what they are. You help your child to recognize that he is upset; you help him to identify the cause and to talk about it. Then you help him to work out ways of overcoming difficulties, and solving problems.

Here is another example:

Ben, aged seven, has started getting stomach aches when he wakes up. On a number of occasions he said he did not feel well enough to go to school.

Ben — Daddy, my stomach's hurting.

Father — Oh, that's too bad.

Ben — Can I stay in bed?

Father — No, you have to go to school.

Ben — I don't want to, my stomach hurts.

Father — Sometimes, my stomach hurts when I'm worried about things.

Ben — I'm not worried, my stomach hurts.

Father — Look, Ben, your stomach hurts only in the mornings when it's time to go to school, and I think something's worrying you about school. Shall I have a guess what it is?

Ben — Don't know.

Father — I'm not sure whether it's lessons, one of the teachers, or the other kids.

Ben — It's none of that.

Father — Come on, Ben – it's okay; when I was a kid there were things at school that upset me too.

Ben — Like what?

Father — I wasn't good at games, and got teased. And my writing was bad and my teacher told me off.

Ben — Mr Carter (his teacher) says I'm stupid, and then the other kids laugh.

Father — When does he say you're stupid.

Ben — 'cos I can't answer some of the questions.

Father — Okay, so of course you get worried about school then. Now I'll have a word with Mr Carter, and this evening you can tell me some more about the questions you can't answer.

Here, Ben's father has recognized that Ben is worried, and has helped him talk about it. He did it by showing that he also got worried, and had had troubles himself at school. In other words, he made no judgments or criticisms, but simply accepted Ben's worries as justified. He then set about working out solutions.

If such techniques do not work, gently persevere for a while. Other things you can do are to play guessing-games about the worries, or tell a story that allows your child to identify with the main character. In this way, he can hear about how someone like him reacted to and coped with a similar problem.

If, despite all your efforts, you still do not succeed, then it is worth seeking help (see Chapter ten).

Being part of a family

Families are complicated. Being part of one, though natural, is not always easy. One aspect of good-enough parenting is helping your child to be part of the family. When very young, your child gets enormous amounts of attention from you. As he gets older you should help him to get used to receiving less. This is all the more the case if another baby is born, or other things happen that take up your time and energy. Mothers and fathers need time to be alone together, or simply alone, and you should help your child to cope with that.

Taking the lead All families have problems to solve, decisions to make, conflicts to resolve. Good-enough parenting involves you taking a lead in these tasks. Children learn to carry out these tasks for themselves when older, seeing how their parents manage them. If you fail to carry out these tasks, then not only do your children not learn for themselves, but they can also suffer when things go wrong as a result. For example, couples who are unable to settle their differences will often involve their children in the conflict. Sometimes a child is asked, openly or in more subtle ways, to take one parent's side against the other.

On other occasions, parents may be distracted from sorting things out because their child draws their attention. Such a child is in danger of carrying an awful burden – that of peace-maker. Some parents even blame their differences on their child; they make him a scapegoat. Obviously, none of this is satisfac-

tory. Parents have to be the most responsible members of a family, and if things go wrong, it is their responsibility to sort it out.

Working together When there are two of you, you should always work things out together. It is very unsatisfactory for one of you to undermine the other; perhaps one of you says your child cannot stay up to watch television and then the other says he can. Children, incidentally, are very skilled at exploiting parental differences, to no one's long term advantage.

If you cannot agree, then you should set aside some time to chat and sort it out. You should make every effort to compromise. If you cannot compromise, then you should at least support each other in your child's presence. It is distressing and confusing for children to be given contradictory messages at the same time. This is not to say that adults should never disagree in front of the children. That would be impossible. Anyhow, children need to see how you disagree and eventually resolve your differences – providing, of course, your disagreements are neither violent or vicious.

Practical tips on good-enough parenting

When you are angry

Bringing up children is tiring and stressful. There are bound to be times when you feel like shouting, screaming or hitting out. If you are feeling angry with your child, it is best to say so, and say why. At times you will feel better for shouting at him, but again try to explain why you have done so. If you feel you really cannot stand what is happening at a particular moment, send him out of the room to cool off. Alternatively, leave the room yourself, to give yourself breathing space.

You are bound to lose control from time to time. All parents do. Most parents smack their children occasionally, especially when the children are younger. Obviously it is better not to smack, but if you do, explain why quickly, and make it up as soon as you can.

If your child is frequently doing things that annoy or worry you, it is best to find a quiet time when you can sit down with him and discuss the problems. A cool calm talk is ten times better than a yell or a smack. Look at the examples of how to discuss problems on pages 98–9; they will illustrate how to set about it, whatever the problem.

Setting an example
It is no use expecting your child not to copy you. Children always copy their parents to some extent. If, for example you swear or smoke, it is almost inevitable that your child will do so eventually as well. If you are very rude to him, he is likely to be rude in return. On the other hand, if you set an example of kindness and concern for others, he is likely to copy that.

All too often parents express concern to me about a particular behaviour in their child, only to show me that one or both of them do exactly the same thing. It is always worth checking whether you are setting the wrong or right example.

Remember, you will often make mistakes because you are human, and not infrequently you will feel frustrated, angry and even resentful. But that is all right because neither you nor your child is perfect. That would be intolerable for everyone else!

If there are problems that you can-

Guidelines for good-enough parenting.

- Be consistent without being rigid
- Be flexible without being chaotic
- Praise and reward rather than ignore and punish
- Make rules that are reasonable
- Be consistent in applying rules
- Be neither overprotective nor underprotective
- Watch for situations that cause stress
- When your child is distressed, acknowledge the problem, comfort him, and try to find ways of helping
- Help your child to adjust to change and eventually to become independent.

not overcome despite doing your very best and following the advice offered in this book, then you should seek help. In the next chapter I discuss how to get help, and what you might expect.

10. WHERE TO SEEK HELP AND WHAT TO EXPECT

Virtually all parents worry about their children's behaviour from time to time. I have tried to show throughout this book what you can do to help your child when various problems arise. It may be, however, that you are unable to carry out the suggestions I have made, or that you have tried them without success. Alternatively, you may be so worried about your child's behaviour or about your family or yourself, that you wish to seek professional advice and help immediately. In this chapter I shall describe where you may get such advice and what sort of help may be offered.

Shying away from help
It is a sad fact that many parents avoid seeking help. Reasons include not wanting to draw attention to their child for fear of being labelled as 'odd' or incompetent, or worrying that the problem will be made worse. In fact, if there are problems it is far better to get them sorted out quickly and effectively. If you have tried yourself without success, it is unlikely that the problems will simply disappear. So do seek help – after all you do want to do what is best for your child. Begin by talking with your family doctor or school psychologist.

Who you might see
It may be helpful to understand the differences between the various professionals you might come across:

Child psychiatrists are fully qualified doctors who have specialized in psychological medicine and have then become further specialized in the emotional and behavioural problems of childhood. They can prescribe medicines, unlike the other professionals mentioned.

Child psychologists have a training in psychology (the study of human behaviour) and then specialize in either educational or clinical psychology.

Educational psychologists (In Australia, School counsellors) have a particular interest in school learning difficulties. They may practice at a school or be affiliated with a school district.

Clinical psychologists have more interest in behavioural and emotional difficulties.

Child psychotherapists have usually been trained in psychology and then developed a particular expertise in the understanding and treatment of deep-rooted emotional difficulties.

Social workers have a general training in such areas as psychology and social welfare. They provide a wide range of services, which might include counselling, advice about how and where to get help with a social problem, and various types of therapy (see page 109).

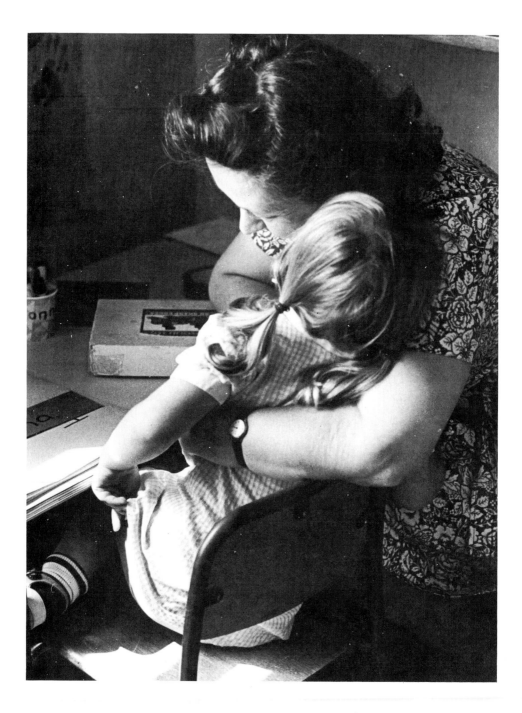

For younger children, drawing and play are an important part of psychotherapy.

Counsellors do not come from any specific professional background but are trained to understand and advise you about educational, personal or marital difficulties. They may be employed in school, general practices or marriage guidance clinics.

Probation officers and Court welfare officers have a similar role to that of social workers but are employed by Courts who can empower them (like social workers) to become involved in the supervision of a child's welfare, for example, when children are the subject of dispute between divorced parents, or when children have broken the law.

Assessments

The nature and depth of the assessment can vary enormously depending upon the type of problem and who you consult. It may be possible to give useful advice on the basis of very little information but sometimes it may be necessary to get very detailed information about the background to the problem, as well as carrying out various tests and perhaps physical examinations. In general it is likely that you will be asked a number of questions about your child's development and the problem that is worrying you. For example, when did he start to walk, talk, be toilet-trained, and so on; and when did the problem start, were there any obvious factors that might have started it? There is no harm in thinking about such questions in advance and noting down details.

The child's background Because a child's problems are so often tied up with family tensions or school difficulties you are likely to be asked about these areas. Some parents feel resentful that their family life should be probed in this way, but most recognize that it is important to know as much as possible about a child's background for the best possible help to be offered. Even when the problem arises from outside the family or is specifically due to something about the child rather than the family, it is the family who are often best placed to help.

The interview Many professionals will want to interview your child alone. This is because it is sometimes easier for children to talk about things that are bothering them to a complete stranger, than it is to their parents. Providing you show your child that you trust the person concerned, he is likely to separate from you without much anxiety. Some professionals might prefer to meet with your whole family rather than seeing your child alone. There are others who like to do both. While it is a good idea to tell your child what might happen and why, it is not at all helpful to tell him what to say or how to behave. Far better to allow whoever is seeing him to use his skill and experience to help your child be himself; in this way the problems are far more readily understood.

Where there is slow development or the possibility of learning difficulties, it is very likely that the psychologist will carry out a psychological assessment or intelligence test (see Chapter four). This form of assessment can last from half-an-hour to up to two hours. It can include a test of general intelligence as well as tests of particular skills such as reading. If there is any question of a medical or physical problem it is very likely that a physical examination will be done. Later, at the hospital, special investigations such as X-rays, blood tests and tracing the activity of the brain by electro-encephalograms are useful aids to

Many professionals prefer to chat to a child alone, others prefer working with the family.

ruling out various physical disorders (see page 45).

Treatments

Many different treatments are available to help children and their families. Here I want to describe briefly the most common forms of treatment. Different problems require different treatments. Some problems are so complex that a combination of treatments are required. So do not be surprised if no immediate or single solution is offered. There may well be a period of observation or a series of tests, which will be followed by one or several kinds of treatment.

Advice and counselling
Most agencies are likely to offer you practical advice on how best to handle the problems causing you concern. Such counselling may involve advising you to do more or less what you are doing or perhaps trying something different. Naturally, all the advice will be tailored to your child's or family's needs and those needs will also govern how long and how often counselling will take place.

The parents of John, aged three, had become very worried by his temper-tantrums which had increased in frequency and severity. They did everything they could to calm him down during these episodes, which often involved giving him something he wanted or removing something he didn't like. The clinic doctor advised them to ignore him completely instead of trying to soothe him during a tantrum, but to give him plenty of attention otherwise. Within a week the tantrums had stopped.

Kerrie, aged eleven, had developed various fears, particularly related to mixing with other children and travelling on public transport. Her parents had been inclined to help her avoid these situations but she seemed to get worse. She had recently started at a new school and her principal suggested they discuss the problem with the educational psychologist. He advised them firstly to insist that Kerrie went to school, and secondly, to go there by bus rather than being taken by car – something that had inconvenienced the family. He explained that the longer something worrying is avoided, the more worrying it becomes. Once the parents were persuaded to follow his advice Kerrie quickly overcame her difficulties.

Changing behaviour patterns

This form of treatment, known as behaviour therapy or modification, is most commonly used by psychologists, although others also use it occasionally. It involves the use of strategies aimed at helping your child change his behaviour. It is based on the idea that most of our behaviour is learned (or conditioned). For example, if your toddler is in danger of hurting himself by, say, going near a fireplace, you remove him from the source of danger and say a firm 'No', or 'Don't'. Soon your toddler learns to avoid danger areas simply by hearing your instruction, and eventually he cautions himself. In this way, you have shaped your child's behaviour.

Many clinics use behaviour modification for a wide range of problems. The example opposite of John and his temper-tantrums illustrated the use of behaviour therapy. John had learned that he received considerable attention from his parents and that he got his way when he had a tantrum. Once his parents ignored the tantrums he received a different message – 'You don't get our attention and you don't get your own way when you have a tantrum'. He learned that nothing was gained from them and so gave them up.

Star charts

A common way of encouraging a certain line of behaviour is the use of star charts and other rewards.

Tyrone, aged six, was fearful of sitting on the toilet. As a result, he tended to soil his pants. His parents were advised to use a reward scheme. Every time he sat on the toilet he received a star, which was placed on a special chart. He was told that when he had ten stars he would get a small present. In this way, he was gradually encouraged to get used to sitting on the toilet. Once he had done this, the scheme was altered, and stars were offered only for actually opening his bowels in the toilet. After a few weeks Tyrone was able to use the toilet properly.

There are endless variations on the use of such reward schemes. To be effective your child has to want the reward, and to start with, rewards should be given often and be easy to earn. As progress is made, rewards can become harder to earn. It is important that you are consistent and enthusiastic when using these schemes, otherwise they are less likely to work.

Some people are critical of reward schemes because they consider them to be little short of bribery and corruption. I do not believe that to be the case. In fact, much if not most of child-rearing is based on 'rewarding' children for doing things you approve

An example of a star chart. Share your enthusiasm for your child's efforts.

of – the happy smile and the 'good boy' are, in fact, rewards for doing something you approve of. In contrast, when your child does something of which you disapprove, you either ignore it if possible, express disapproval if necessary, and punish if really essential. All this is behaviour modification, and plays an essential part in bringing up children. An added value of the scheme is that you can use it yourself at home, in direct response to the problems your child has.

A slightly different technique is that used in the 'bell and pad' or 'buzzer' treatment of bed-wetting (see page 31). The alarm goes off just as wetting starts. The body learns to associate waking up with the bladder being full. Soon it is not necessary to have the alarm, because the child wakes automatically.

A final example of behaviour modification is that illustrated in Kerrie's case (on page 107). Fears can be self-perpetuating. The more your child avoids something he fears the worse the fear becomes. Behaviour therapy involves getting rid of the fear by facing and overcoming it. Encouraging your child to go through his fear, rather than avoiding it, is the quickest way of overcoming such problems.

Psychotherapy (or 'talking treatment')

This involves a psychotherapist (or possibly a psychiatrist or psychologist) seeing your child on a regular basis, usually about once a week, for a period which may vary from a few months to as long as two or even three years. The aim is to help your child understand what is troubling him and to overcome his problems. For younger children, drawing and play are used, whereas for older children talking about the difficulties is usually possible.

Psychoanalysis

This is basically a more intensive form of psychotherapy and is very rarely used for children. It involves daily treatment sessions, and tends to be very expensive. As there isn't any evidence that psychoanalysis is any more useful than any other treatments its expense and time cannot really be justified.

Family therapy

As the name suggests, this is a treatment that involves the whole family. Family therapy recognizes that however your child's problems may have arisen, the family is the best place to help him overcome them. It is of course also possible that the way a family handles the problem may make it worse. This makes it all the more useful to involve all of you in the treatment. The family therapist (who may be a psychiatrist, psychologist, social worker or psychotherapist) discusses with your family the problems and helps you to find ways of overcoming them. You will all be seen around every two weeks, and the treatment may involve anything from one to a dozen meetings. It is a particularly useful treatment when there are difficulties in your family's relationships.

Carol, aged twelve, suffered from frequent stomach aches for which the doctors could find no physical cause. As most such pains in childhood are the result of tension, she was referred to a child psychiatrist who arranged to meet the whole family. The family consisted of the two parents, both in their forties, Carol, Laura, aged fourteen, and Alan, aged two. The father was always very busy, having to work overtime, and the mother had for the last three years been preoccupied with Alan. Laura was an extrovert girl who had many interests and friends. Carol in contrast was quiet and a bit of a loner. In consequence, she had become quite isolated, and obviously unhappy. Her parents had not been able to recognize her unhappiness and it was only when she developed her stomach aches that they realized something was wrong.

The family therapist helped the family recognize not only that the stomach aches represented Carol's distress, but also that the family had become rather fragmented – father and Laura busy in their own ways, mother and Alan very close, which left Carol on her own. They realized that they had gradually slipped into this pattern, and decided to change things. After three family meetings the situation had improved considerably. The parents were spending more time with Carol and Laura, they had had some family outings and Alan was beginning to get absorbed in his toys and could play alone for reasonable lengths of time. Carol's pains had gone.

Warning signal Families do frequently get into difficulties without recognizing why it has happened, or sometimes even that they are in difficulties. It is the behaviour or ill-health of one of the children that is the warning signal. Family therapy helps families recognize such patterns, often identifies the cause, and aims to help families change their attitudes or their routines so that the situation improves.

Marital therapy

In marital therapy, which is similar to family therapy, only the two adults are involved. It is most useful when you are having difficulties with your marriage and both of you want help. It is also valuable when your children are obviously worried about your troubles. Under these circumstances, whoever is advising you about your child's problems may recommend that you have some help with your marriage. Treatment may last from a few weeks to several months.

Even if one partner refused to accept such help, it is still possible to have marriage guidance (or counselling). The main difference is that in marital therapy the couple work together to overcome their difficulties, assisted by the therapist. In marriage guidance or counselling, which can be with one or both partners, the counsellor tends to be more directive, offering advice and ideas.

It is not surprising that once the marriage improves so does the child's difficult behaviour and emotional distress. If, therefore, you are having marital problems that could be affecting your child, do not hesitate to seek help from any of the professionals mentioned who offer marital therapy.

Medicines

On the whole, there is very little place for medicines in the treatment of children's behaviour problems. There are a few conditions, however, in which certain medicines have some value.

Sleeping medicines are useful in the management of severe sleep disturbance in very young children (see page 20). A small dose used for short periods can help break a faulty sleep pattern, and also give you a valuable night's sleep at a point when you might be despairing. Promethazine and trimeprazine are safe and therefore the best choice. They are not in the least bit addictive, but nevertheless should only be given on doctor's advice. Older children should not be given medicines for sleep problems but encouraged to find some other way of getting to sleep or otherwise occupying themselves.

Tranquillizers such as diazepam should only be used very rarely. Extremely anxious children may benefit from their use, but other treatments should always be tried first. Stronger tranquillizers such as chlorpromazine or haloperidol do have unpleasant side-effects, such as drowsiness, restlessness, or stiffness. They are used only for very seriously disturbed children, for hyperactive children (see Chapter three) and occasionally for severe tics (see page 37).

Antidepressants such as imipramine or amitriptyline are used in two conditions:

1. Bed-wetting (see page 17) is often relieved while one of these medicines is being used. This is not because bed-wetters are depressed but because the drug affects the bladder.
2. True depression (see page 65) is rare in childhood. When it does occur antidepressants can

be most helpful. They can have unpleasant side-effects (such as drowsiness, dizziness, dry mouth, constipation), so should be used sparingly.

A relatively new medicine, lithium, is being found increasingly helpful in a number of areas. In particular, it seems useful when children get very depressed frequently, and when they have severe mood swings. It may also be helpful for aggressive children if the aggression is associated with mood swings. Blood samples must be taken to make sure the right amount of lithium is in the blood and the dosage altered to keep it to a certain level.

Very rarely, a medicine called methylphenidate is used to help children who find it very difficult to give their attention to anything and who are usually also extremely overactive (see Chapter three). It is helpful in these conditions but can have side-effects such as stomach aches. If used for more than a few months it can delay growth, so it is best used for short spells only.

When taking medicines If your child is treated with any of these medicines do stick to the instructions about dosage and how often they are to be taken. Otherwise, they may not work, and it is harder for the doctor to weigh up their usefulness. Store them in a cool, dark place. Report any side-effects to your doctor, so that he can, if necessary, adjust the dose. It is better that you supervise the taking of any of these medicines. In this way, you can be certain that they are being used properly. This even applies to teenagers up to about the age of sixteen.

In general, medicines should always be used in conjunction with one or more of the other treatments mentioned in this chapter. Rarely do they remove the cause of the problem, but occasionally they calm down the problems when used appropriately, and so allow a vicious circle to be broken. In this way, other forms of treatment are then more effective.

EPILOGUE AND USEFUL ADDRESSES

Having read this book, you will now be aware that it is quite normal for parents to have worries about their children and for children to be difficult and worrying from time to time. You will know also that when such problems arise it is worth trying to understand how your child is feeling, and why. You may have tried the various strategies designed to help you and your child through the difficult patch. If these have failed you may decide to seek help from an expert, who will hopefully be able to make life easier. You should never be ashamed of seeking help for, in the end, what matters most is that your child should be healthy and happy. I have included below some useful addresses of various support groups and organizations, to supplement the help you can get from your family doctor, child guidance clinic and other agencies mentioned in Chapter 10.

UNITED KINGDOM

Al-anon Family Groups
61 Great Dover Street
London SE1 4YF

Anorexics Anonymous
24 Westmoreland Road
Barnes
London SW13

Cheyne Holiday Club for Handicapped Children
61 Cheyne Walk
Chelsea
London SW3

Child Poverty Action Group
1 Macklin Street
Drury Lane
London WC2B 5NH

Hyperactive Children's Support Group
59 Meadowside
Angmering
West Sussex

Invalid Children's Aid Association
126 Buckingham Palace Road
London SW1W 9SB

Mind (National Association for Mental Health)
22 Harley Street
London W1N 2ED

National Association for the Welfare of Children in Hospital
Exton House
7 Exton Street
London SE1

National Autistic Society
276 Willesden Lane
London NW2

UNITED STATES

Administration for Children
  Youth and Families
PO Box 1182
Washington
DC 20013

Administration on Developmental
  Disabilities HHS
Office of Human Development
  Services
Room 340E HHH Building
200 Independence Avenue SW
Washington
DC 20201

American Academy of Child
  Psychiatry
3615 Wisconsin Avenue NW
Washington
DC 20016

American Association of
  Psychiatric Services for Children
Suite 1112
1725 K Street NW
Washington
DC 20006

Foundation for Children with
  Learning Disabilities
PO Box 2929
Grand Central Station
New York
NY 10163

National Clearinghouse for Child
  Abuse and Neglect
PO Box 1182
Washington
DC 20013

National Easter Seal Society
2023 West Ogden Avenue
Chicago
Il 60612

National Information Center for
  Handicapped Children and
  Youth
PO Box 1492
Washington
DC 20013

Orton Dyslexia Society
724 York Road
Baltimore
MD 21204

CANADA

Canadian Association for Children
  with Learning Disabilities
Kildaire House
323 Chapel Street
Ottawa, ON
K1G 3Y6

Canadian Institute of Child
  Health
17 York Street
Suite 202
Ottawa, ON
K1N 5S7

Canadian Medical Association
1867 Alta Vista Drive
Ottawa, ON
K1G 3Y6

Canadian Paediatric Society
Centre hospitalier universitaire de
  Sherbrooke
Sherbrooke, PQ
J1H 5N4

Family Service Association of
  Metropolitan Toronto
22 Wellesley Street E
Toronto, ON
M4Y 1G3

The Institute of Family Living
120 Eglinton Avenue E
Toronto, ON
M4P 1E2

Society for Emotionally Disturbed
  Children
1622 Sherbrook Street W
3rd Floor
Montreal, PQ
H3H 1C9

Toughlove Parent Support Group
11 Nevada Avenue
Willowdale, ON
M2M 3N9

INTERNATIONAL DRUG-NAME EQUIVALENTS

Generic name	UK trade name	Australia trade name
amitriptyline	Tryptizol Elavil Saroten Domical	Amitrip Laroxyl Saroten Tryptanol
chlorpromazine	Largactil Chloractil	Largactil Protran
diazepam	Valium Atensine Evacalm Solis Tensium etc.	Valium Ducene Pro-Pam
dicyclomine	Merbentyl	Merbentyl
haloperidol	Serenace Haldol Fortunan	Serenace Pacedol
imipramine	Tofranil Praminil	Tofranil Imiprin
lithium	Camcolit Priadel Liskonum Phasal Litarex	Camcolit Priadel Lithicarb Carbolith
methylphenidate	Ritalin	Ritalin
promethazine	Phenergan	Phenergan Meth-Zine
thioridazine	Melleril	Melleril
trimeprazine	Vallergan	Vallergan

Generic name	US trade name	Canada trade name
amitriptyline	Elavil Amitid Endep SK-Amitriptyline	Elavil Meravil Levate Novotriptyn
chlorpromazine	Thorazine	Largactil Novochlorpromazine
diazepam	Valium	Valium E-Pam Meval Novodipam Neo-Calme Rival etc.
dicyclomine	Bentyl	Bentylol Lomine etc.
haloperidol	Haldol	Haldol Peridol
imipramine	Tofranil Janimine	Trofranil Impril etc.
lithium	Eskalith Lithane Lithonate Lithotabs	Carbolith Lithane Lithizine
methylphenidate	Ritalin	Ritalin
promethazine	Phenergan Remsed	Phenergan Histantil
thioridazine	Mellaril	Mellaril Thioril etc.
trimeprazine	Temaril	Panectyl

ACKNOWLEDGEMENTS

I would like to thank Rita Nani, as ever for her patience, efficiency and good humour, while typing the various drafts of this book, and for gently pointing out my many errors and omissions; Piers Murray Hill for his invaluable editorial advice and encouragement; my colleagues at Great Ormond Street Hospital for their friendship and support; my own children, Gideon and Adam, for being so patient with me while I was working on this book; and all the children and their families (their anonymity must be preserved) who, through my contact with them, have taught me so much.

Bryan Lask, 1985

The publishers would like to thank the following for their help in the preparation of this book:

For permission to reproduce photographs, Ace Photo Agency (page 95); the Department of Medical Photography, The Hospital for Sick Children, Great Ormond Street (page 55); Pictor International (cover photograph and pages 6, 9, 28, 81, 134); Zefa Picture Library (page 18); Vision International (page 39).

The photographs on pages 145 and 152 were taken by Ray Moller, assisted by Sharon Lowery.

The International Drug Tables were compiled by Jennifer Eaton.

The diagrams were drawn by David Gifford.

INDEX

Page numbers in *italic* refer to the illustrations.

Court welfare officers, 105
cruelty, 72
'crushes', 71
crying, 49, 65–6, 78
'cuddlies', 23, 24

dark, fear of, 23
deafness, 54, 57
death, child's reaction to, 88, 91–3
deceitfulness, 68
delayed development, 49–60
delayed reactions, 89
delinquency, 80
demand-feeding, 20
dentists, fear of, 65
depression, 46–7, 65–7, 72, 75, 111
deprived children, 58
developmental problems, 49–60
diabetes, 13, 54, 78, 82
diarrhoea, 18, 33–4
diazepam, 25, 26, 111
dicyclomine, 22
diet, and constipation, 32, 34; and
    hyperkinesis, 45–6; and mental
    handicap, 56; see also feeding
    problems
dieting, 86
dishonesty, 68
divorce, 93
doctors, discussing problems with,
    103; fear of, 65
dogs, fear of, 64
Down's syndrome, 55
drinking, alcohol, 73
drug abuse, 73–4, 75; 73
drug experimentation, 73–4
dummies, 23
dyslexia, 11, 59, 69
dysphasia, 58

ear infections, 54, 57
eczema, 78, 80, 82
education welfare officers, 104
educational psychologists, 104
'elective mutism', 62–3
electroencephalograms (EEG), 44,
    106; 44
emotional problems, 59–60; and
    delayed development, 49;
    mothers, 17; and obesity, 85, 86;

psychosomatic problems, 82–3;
    and soiling, 33; toddlers, 20
emotions, 79–80; relationships in
    family life, 96
encephalitis, 47, 54, 56
encopresis (soiling), 33, 34–6
endocrine disorders, 85
enemas, 34
energetic children, 41–7
enuresis, see bed-wetting
epilepsy, 13, 54, 56, 82
excitement, 46–7

family difficulties, 12, 13
family life, 96, 100
Family Service Unit, 104
family therapy, 39, 87, 109–10
Family Welfare Agency, 104
fantasizing, 68
fat, metabolism, 85
fear, 62, 64–5, 78, 109
feeding problems, 15–21; see also
    diet
feelings, bottled-up, 80–1, 83
fits, 38, 46, 47
food allergy, 43, 45–6, 83, 84
food fads, 15, 18, 20
forceps delivery, 47, 48, 56
frustration, 37–8

glandular disorders, 85
'glue ear', 57
glue-sniffing, 73; 73
grief, 92–3

habits, worrying, 36–9
hair-pulling, 36, 37, 39
haloperidol, 39, 45, 111
handicapped children, 13, 54–6
hard drugs, 73
head-banging, 36, 37
head injuries, 47, 54, 56
headaches, 78, 79, 80, 89, 99
health visitors, 103
hearing-aids, 57
hearing tests, 57
heroin, 73
high blood-pressure, 78
homosexuality, 71
horses, fear of, 64–5